WALKING
BERLIN

WALKING

BERLIN

THE BEST OF THE CITY

Paul Sullivan

NATIONAL GEOGRAPHIC

Washington, D.C.

WALKING

BERLIN

CONTENTS

PART **1**

PAGE 12
WHIRLWIND TOURS

PART **2**

PAGE 46
BERLIN'S
NEIGHBORHOODS

PART **3**

PAGE 172
TRAVEL ESSENTIALS

**Previous pages:
Alexanderplatz;
left: Hackesche
Höfe; right: statue
at Jagdschloss
Grunewald; above
right: East Side
Gallery; bottom
right: Reichstag**

Johannes Brix-Berlin

Introduction

I moved to Berlin nine years ago for the cheap rents and edgy art, music scene, and relaxed vibe. Equally important: I was excited to live in a place where past and present collide everywhere you look.

Few cities have lived as many lives as Berlin. In a scant century, the city's been an imperial capital, a synonym for decadence, and a Nazi stronghold. Bombed, invaded, occupied. Suddenly divided, unexpectedly reunited, once again made the capital of a unified Germany.

You can see it all on Unter den Linden, the avenue that runs through the heart of the city's eastern half: Start under the TV tower, an East German icon. In the park below, snap a selfie with statues of Marx and Engels, the architects of a system Germans eagerly discarded 25 years ago. Head west past the Habsburg-era Berlin Cathedral, still scarred by the bombs of World War II, and Humboldt University, where Albert Einstein once taught. Pass through the famous Brandenburg Gate—used as a triumphal arch by Napoleon and Hitler—and cross over the narrow line of bricks that marks the course of the Berlin Wall. Finally, take in the glittering glass dome atop the stolid gray stone of the Reichstag.

Locals relax over a glass of Berliner Pilsner in the leafy Schleusenkrug beer garden in the city's popular Tiergarten park.

Using this guide, remember—the German capital is no museum, though it has plenty of them. A quarter-century after the fall of the Berlin Wall, the city's become an oasis for creative types of every stripe. Berlin's intriguing, often difficult history hasn't kept it from embracing the present and pursuing the future.

Andrew Curry
National Geographic Traveler writer and Berlin-based foreign correspondent

Visiting Berlin

Since the fall of the Berlin Wall in 1989, Berlin has undergone a rapid, yet considered, program of regeneration. Focused on the historical center, the once-divided city is now whole again. What you see is a thriving cultural capital that nevertheless remains studded with fascinating glimpses into its turbulent past.

Berlin in a Nutshell

Berlin's historic center straddles the Spree River, which flows from east to west through the city. Radiating out from here are a number of neighborhoods, each with its own distinct characteristics. They include buzzy Kreuzberg to the south, gritty Friedrichshain to the east, and leafy Tiergarten to the west. Each of these neighborhoods—and others featured in this book—offers a diverse range of sights and is well worth a day's visit in its own right. Much of what now comprises central Berlin lay behind the Berlin Wall in the former German Democratic Republic (GDR) – in German, the *Deutsche Demokratische Republik (DDR),* and remnants of the Cold War years abound.

Berlin Day-by-Day

Open every day With some exceptions for major public holidays, almost all sites are open every day.

Monday All sites open except AlliiertenMuseum, Alte Nationalgalerie, Altes Museum, Bode-Museum, Deutsche Kinemathek, Deutsches Technikmuseum, Gemäldegalerie, Jagdschloss Grunewald, Knoblauchhaus, Neue Nationalgalerie, Schloss Charlottenburg. Also, Berlinische Galerie is free entry on first Monday of the month; Jüdisches Museum is open until 9 p.m.; visitor center at Gedenkstätte Berliner Mauer is closed.

Tuesday All sites open except Bauhaus-Archiv, Haus der Kulturen der Welt (exhibitions only), Berlinische Galerie

Wednesday All sites open except Jagdschloss Grunewald

Thursday All sites open except Jagdschloss Grunewald. All Museumsinsel institutions are open until 8 p.m.

Friday All sites open except Jagdschloss Grunewald.

Saturday/Sunday All sites open.

Tourists enjoy a cruise on the Spree River between Museumsinsel and Monbijoupark.

VISITING BERLIN

Navigating Berlin

With the vast majority of key sights in or around the historic center of Berlin, the core of the city is easily navigated on foot. There is also an extremely efficient public transportation network that makes good use of frequent buses *(Busse)*, trams *(Strassenbahnen)*, and trains. These operate both underground *(U-Bahn)* and overground *(S-Bahn)* for swift access to those sights that lie farther afield. Before setting out, arm yourself with a detailed street map of the city and its transportation network, available from Berlin's tourist authority (see p. 177).

Enjoying Berlin for Less

Berlin is *the* city of discounts—either on public transportation, for entry to key tourist sights, or for eating and drinking in numerous establishments. By far the best deals are to be had with the **Berlin WelcomeCard** (see p. 175), available for various lengths of stay. Some cards come with free public transportation for up to three children. All WelcomeCards include 25 to 50 percent discounts on more than 200 cultural sights and restaurants, and are issued with free street maps and network plans for public transportation.

Using This Guide

Each tour—which might be only a walk, or might take advantage of the city's public transportation as well—is plotted on a map and has been planned to take into account opening hours and the times of day when sites are less crowded. Many end near restaurants or lively nightspots for evening activities.

Whirlwind Tours

Whirlwind Tours are for people who have only a day or a weekend to spend in the city and want to be sure that they see the very best. Choose your tour based on your time and interests: One Day; Weekend; For Fun; For Spies; For Contemporary Architecture Fans; and With Kids.

Tips For the Day and Weekend Tours, a Tips spread following the itinerary map provides insider information on detours from the key sites, extra places to see, nearby cafés and restaurants, and ideas for adapting the tours to suit your interests.

Site Descriptions
In the For Fun, For Spies, For Contemporary Architecture Fans, and With Kids tours, key sites spreads following the maps provide descriptions of all the sites and necessary practical information for visitors.

Neighborhood Tours

The seven neighborhood tours each begin with an introduction, followed by an itinerary map highlighting the key sites that make up the tour and detailed key sites descriptions. Each tour is followed by an "in-depth" spread showcasing one major site along the route, a "distinctly" Berlin spread providing background information on a quintessential element of that neighborhood, and a "best of" spread that groups sites thematically.

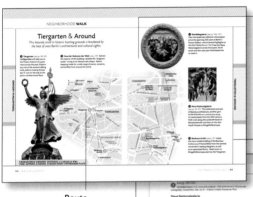

Itinerary Map A map of the neighborhood shows the locations of the key sites, U- and S-Bahn stations, and main streets.

Captions These briefly describe the key sites and give instructions on finding the next site on the tour. Page references direct you to full descriptions of the key sites on the following pages.

Route
Dotted lines link the key sites.

Price Ranges for Key Sites

€	Less than €4
€€	€4–€8
€€€	€8–€13
€€€€	€13–€18
€€€€€	More than €18

Price Ranges for Good Eats (for one person, excluding drinks)

€	Less than €15
€€	€15–€25
€€€	€25–€40
€€€€	€40–€60
€€€€€	More than €60

Key Sites Descriptions These provide a detailed description and highlights for each site, following the order on the map, plus its address, website, phone number, entrance fee, days closed, and nearest U- or S-Bahn station.

Good Eats Refer to these lists for a selection of cafés and restaurants.

PART 1

Whirlwind Tours

Berlin in a Day

*The compelling story of Berlin's complex history unfolds
on this packed tour of the city's must-see sights.*

8 Potsdamer Platz
(see pp. 56–57) Marvel at
the skyscrapers in this
masterpiece of 21st-century
urban planning, before
sampling the delights of one of
its many bars and restaurants.

6 Tiergarten (see pp. 98–99) Explore
the many paths of central Berlin's
largest green space. Dotted with
sculptures and memorials today, the
park once served as a royal hunting
ground. Cross Ebertstrasse.

7 Holocaust Monument
(see p. 55) Pause to
reflect at this powerful
memorial. Walk south
on Ebertstrasse.

5 Reichstag (see pp. 62–63)
Follow the spiral walkway to
the top of the glass dome and
a bird's-eye view over Berlin.
Cross Scheidemannstrasse and
head into the Tiergarten.

4 Brandenburger Tor
(see p. 54) You'll see the
Brandenburg Gate as you
approach Pariser Platz. Pass
beneath the winged goddess
of victory and head north
on Ebertstrasse.

Map labels:
- Hauptbahnhof
- LUISENSTRASSE
- KAPELLE-UFER
- SPREEBOGEN-PARK
- Bundestag
- Berlin Wall Memorial
- Memorial to Sinti and Roma Victims of National Socialism
- **5 Reichstag**
- REGIERUNGS VIERTEL
- Haus der Kulturen der Welt
- Brandenburg Tor
- **Brandenburger Tor 4**
- ← To Siegessäule
- STRASSE DES 17. JUNI
- **Tiergarten 6**
- Holocaust Monument
- **7**
- Memorial to Homosexuals Persecuted under Nazism
- TIERGARTENTUNNEL
- VOSSSTRASSE
- Sony Center
- LEIPZIGER PLATZ
- Potsdamer Platz
- **Potsdamer Platz 8**
- Potsdamer Platz
- POTSDAMER STR.
- MARLENE-DIETRICH-PLATZ
- LINKSTRASSE
- TILLA-DURIEUX-PARK
- KÖTHENER STR
- STRESEMANN
- SCHÖNEBERGER
- ASKANISCHER PLATZ
- Mendelssohn-Bartholdy-Park
- Anhalter Bahnhof
- MENDELSSOHN-BARTHOLDY-PARK
- UFER
- Gleisdreieck
- Möckernbrücke

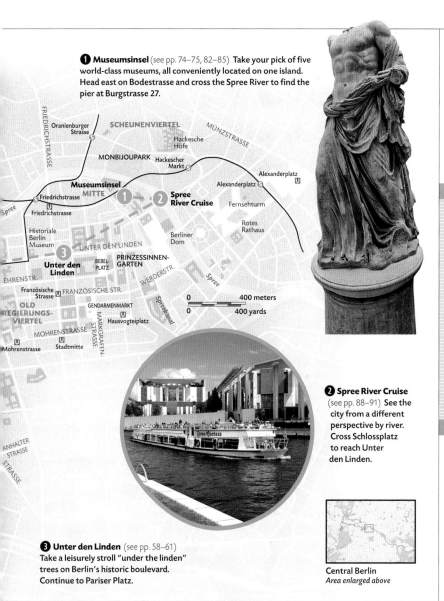

❶ Museumsinsel (see pp. 74–75, 82–85) **Take your pick of five world-class museums, all conveniently located on one island. Head east on Bodestrasse and cross the Spree River to find the pier at Burgstrasse 27.**

❷ Spree River Cruise (see pp. 88–91) **See the city from a different perspective by river. Cross Schlossplatz to reach Unter den Linden.**

❸ Unter den Linden (see pp. 58–61) Take a leisurely stroll "under the linden" trees on Berlin's historic boulevard. Continue to Pariser Platz.

Central Berlin
Area enlarged above

Tips

This tour offers the best of the sights in Berlin. Each is described elsewhere in the book—just follow the cross-references for more detailed information. The following tips provide advice on visiting these major locations when you have limited time and also suggest additional sights nearby and places to eat.

WHIRLWIND TOURS

❶ Museumsinsel (see pp. 74–75, 82–85) Arrive early to avoid the crowds, especially in summer. If you don't plan on getting a ■ BERLIN WELCOMECARD AND MUSEUM ISLAND PASS (see p. 175), you can beat the hoardes by buying in advance online (www.smb.museum). Tickets are often cheaper this way, too. Despite their proximity to one another, it would be exhausting to visit all five museums in a day, so focus on just one.

❷ Spree River Cruise (see pp. 88–91) Glide through Berlin's historic city center on a one-hour boat tour with ■ BERLINER WASSERSPORT- UND SERVICE GMBH & CO. (BWSG; see p. 88). From the water, you will get a different perspective on Museumsinsel, as well as see a number of other primary sights such as the ■ REGIERUNGSVIERTEL (Berlin's ultramodern Government Quarter). Boats depart every 30 minutes.

❸ Unter den Linden (see pp. 58–61) If you have time for an entertaining overview of the capital's turbulent past, "Berlin in One Hour" at the ■ HISTORIALE BERLIN MUSEUM (Unter den Linden 40, www.historiale.de) offers a photographic re-creation of some of the city's most famous scenes.

❹ Brandenburger Tor (see p. 54) Seeking refreshment? Admire the Brandenburg Gate from a distance on the terrace of ■ HOTEL ADLON (Unter den Linden 77), the celebrity hot spot of the Weimar years (see pp. 64–67). You'll pass the hotel as you approach the gate from Unter den Linden. If it's raining, step inside and enjoy a tipple at the hotel's decadent lounge bar instead.

❺ Reichstag (see pp. 62–63) Visitors to the dome are admitted every 15 minutes. Buy tickets online ahead of your trip to secure a time slot to suit your

Hotel Adlon, Pariser Platz

itinerary *(www.bundestag.de)*. If you plan to visit the Reichstag in the evening (see Customizing Your Day), take a stroll through the ribbon of official structures that comprises the ■ REGIERUNGSVIERTEL (Government Quarter) to find the ■ BERLIN WALL MEMORIAL that includes some original segments.

❻ Tiergarten (see pp. 98–99) If time is short, confine your visit to the eastern flank of this park, which contains two World War II memorials. Directly across from the southern edge of the Reichstag is the ■ MEMORIAL TO SINTI AND ROMA VICTIMS OF NATIONAL SOCIALISM, a round water basin with a triangular stone stele supporting a single flower at its center. Farther south, near Lennéstrasse, is the ■ MEMORIAL TO HOMOSEXUALS PERSECUTED UNDER NAZISM (see p. 55). If you've time for a breezy stroll, pick any of the paths leading to the ■ SIEGESSÄULE (Victory Column; see p. 98) on Strasse des 17. Juni, and back before moving on.

❼ Holocaust Monument (see p. 55) Early evening is the best time to visit this monument. Although it can be accessed all hours, most tourists will have left by now. A certain stillness descends toward the end of the day, allowing you to experience the full impact of the memorial's somewhat disorienting design without distraction from others.

❽ Potsdamer Platz (see pp. 56–57) Round off your day watching the sun set from the terrace bar at the top of ■ KOLLHOFF-TOWER (*Alte Potsdamer Strasse 7*) or dine on elegant German-Austrian cuisine at ■ LUTTER & WEGNER (*Alte Potsdamer Strasse 5*).

CUSTOMIZING **YOUR DAY**

One of the most pleasant ways to enjoy the Reichstag is to book dinner at the **Käfer** rooftop restaurant (see p. 63; *last entry 10 p.m.*). Satisfy yourself with the river view of the building in the morning and skip the Reichstag visit in the afternoon. If you take this option, it makes sense to swap the last two sights of the day. See p. 25 for more options at Potsdamer Platz.

Berlin in a Weekend

*This compact tour of Berlin's most-visited landmarks
starts with a cruise on the Spree River.*

| 0 | | 400 meters |
| 0 | | 400 yards |

Hauptbahnhof

KANZLERGARTEN
Bundeskanzleramt

Haus der
Kulturen
der Welt

STRASSE DES 17. JUN

TIERGARTEN

BELLEVUEALLEE

TIERGARTENSTRASSE

KULTUR-
FORUM

Gemälde-
galerie

Neue
National-
galerie

❶ **Spree River Cruise** (see pp. 88–91)
Relax on this leisurely cruise of the
city's main sights. Heading west, cross
Museumsinsel on Bodestrasse and
walk south on Am Kupfergraben,
flanking the Spreekanal.

❷ **Unter den Linden**
(see pp. 74–75, 82–85)
Head west on this grand
boulevard. You'll see
an equestrian statue
of Frederick the Great
on the way. With the
Brandenburg Gate in
sight, make your way
to Pariser Platz.

❸ **Brandenburger Tor**
(see p. 54) Pass through the gate
to Ebertstrasse, shaking hands
with the Berlin Bear if you're lucky
enough to spot him. Head south.

❹ **Holocaust Monument**
(see p. 55) Visit the Ort der
Information (Information Center)
at the southeastern corner of this
memorial for a sobering tribute to
the Jewish victims of the Holocaust.

**BERLIN IN A WEEKEND DAY 1 DISTANCE: 2 MILES (3.2 KM)
TIME: APPROX. 6 HOURS S-BAHN START: HACKESCHER MARKT**

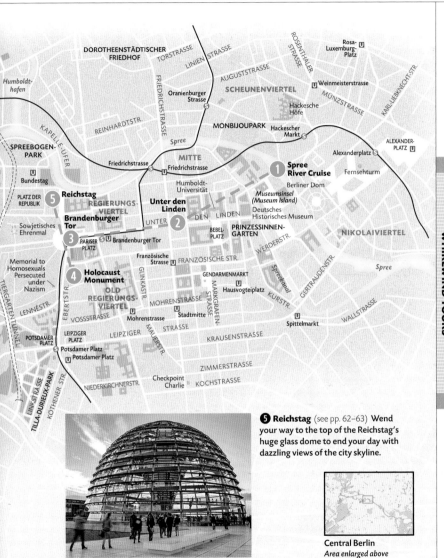

DOROTHEENSTÄDTISCHER FRIEDHOF

TORSTRASSE

LINIENSTRASSE

AUGUSTSTRASSE

ROSENTHALER STRASSE

Rosa-
Luxemburg-
Platz

Humboldt-
hafen

FRIEDRICHSTRASSE

Oranienburger
Strasse

SCHEUNENVIERTEL

Weinmeisterstrasse

MÜNZSTRASSE

KARL-LIEBKNECHT-STR.

REINHARDTSTR.

Hackesche
Höfe

MONBIJOUPARK

Hackescher
Markt

KAPELLE-UFER

Spree

MITTE

SPREEBOGEN-
PARK

Friedrichstrasse

Friedrichstrasse

ALEXANDER-
PLATZ

Alexanderplatz

Bundestag

Humboldt-
Universität

1 **Spree
River Cruise**

Fernsehturm

PLATZ DER
REPUBLIK

5 **Reichstag**

REGIERUNGS-
VIERTEL

**Brandenburger
Tor**

Sowjetisches
Ehrenmal

**Unter den
Linden**

UNTER DEN LINDEN

Berliner Dom

Museumsinsel
(Museum Island)

Deutsches
Historisches Museum

2

BEBEL-
PLATZ

PRINZESSINNEN-
GARTEN

NIKOLAIVIERTEL

Spree

PARISER
PLATZ

Brandenburger Tor

Memorial to
Homosexuals
Persecuted
under
Nazism

4 **Holocaust
Monument**

Französische
Strasse

FRANZÖSISCHE STR.

WERDERSTR.

GERTRAUDENSTR.

OLD
REGIERUNGS-
VIERTEL

GENDARMENMARKT

Hausvogteiplatz

Spreekanal

TIERGARTENTUNNEL

LENNESTR.

GLINKASTR.

VOSSSTRASSE

MOHRENSTRASSE

MARKGRAFEN-
STRASSE

KURSTR.

WALLSTRASSE

EBERTSTR.

Mohrenstrasse

Stadtmitte

STRASSE

Spittelmarkt

POTSDAMER
PLATZ

LEIPZIGER
PLATZ

LEIPZIGER

MAUERSTR.

KRAUSENSTRASSE

Potsdamer Platz

Potsdamer Platz

ZIMMERSTRASSE

LINKSTRASSE

TILLA-DURIEUX-PARK

KÖTHENER STR.

NIEDERKIRCHNERSTR.

Checkpoint
Charlie

KOCHSTRASSE

5 **Reichstag** (see pp. 62–63) Wend
your way to the top of the Reichstag's
huge glass dome to end your day with
dazzling views of the city skyline.

Central Berlin
Area enlarged above

Tips

Two days in Berlin affords enough time to get a true sense of this city's incredible diversity. Day One may appear relatively relaxed, but there is plenty of scope for improvisation. Read up about these sights' main attractions later in the book and consider the following tips for interesting alternatives and detours on the way.

WHIRLWIND TOURS

❶ **Spree River Cruise** (see pp. 88–91) The best way to get an overview of the city in a very short time, this cruise makes an ideal start to your weekend break. Join a round-trip river cruise run by ■ BERLINER WASSERSPORT- UND SERVICE GMBH & CO. (BWSG; see p. 88). Boats depart every 30 minutes, and cruises last an hour. Morning cruises tend to be less busy than afternoon ones, and it is worth booking online in advance

Browsing bookstalls at Humboldt University

(*www.bwsg-berlin.de*) to avoid disappointment in summer.

❷ **Unter den Linden** (see pp. 74–75, 82–85) As you stroll from the east end of this grand boulevard to the west, seek out a couple of courtyards rarely discovered by tourists. The first is at Berlin's seat of learning, ■ HUMBOLDT-UNIVERSITÄT (*No. 6*), whose previous students include Albert Einstein and Karl Marx. On most days, you'll find locals browsing a secondhand book market held here (*times vary*). Next door, at the ■ STAATSBIBLIOTHEK ZU BERLIN (*No. 8*), a courtyard at the Berlin branch of the state library offers shady benches on which to seek a few minutes respite from the heat and the boulevard hordes in summer. If you're seeking refreshment, head to any one of a number of cafés that line the boulevard. Among Berlin's most treasured is the venerable ■ Café Einstein *(Unter den Linden 42)*, with its classic Viennese interior. You'll find it just before the intersection with Glinkastrasse.

❸ Brandenburger Tor (see p. 54)
The Brandenburg Gate is one of the city's most visited sights and busy at almost any time of day. If your arrival coincides with a bus tour (or two) seek a moment's peace in the less publicized ■ Room of Silence on the northern side of the gate. Or pass through the gate and into the ■ Tiergarten (see pp. 98–99) for a leafy detour through the eastern end of Berlin's largest park. A short walk on Strasse des 17. Juni will bring you to the ■ Sowjetisches Ehrenmal (see p. 99) commemorating the Soviet victory over the Nazis in the Battle of Berlin. Also at this end of the park—opposite the Holocaust Monument (see below)— is the ■ Memorial to Homosexuals Persecuted under Nazism (see p. 55). You can exit the park on Ebertstrasse to return to the tour.

❹ Holocaust Monument
(see p. 55) The Holocaust Monument is one of the best known tourist attractions in Berlin, yet not all visitors discover the 8,600-square-foot (800 sq m) ■ Ort der Information (Information Center) below ground. The center

CUSTOMIZING **YOUR DAY**

A Spree River cruise may be less appealing in the colder months, and there is a short period *(mid-Nov.–mid-March)* when there is no service. Opt instead to start the day at the **Deutsches Historisches Museum** (German Historical Museum; see p. 60) at the eastern end of Unter den Linden—to see either the permanent galleries or the museum's temporary exhibition. Alternatively, treat yourself to brunch at the nearby **Café im Deutschen Historischen Museum** (see p. 68).

features four rooms showing personal documentation about Jewish individuals and families murdered by the Nazis.

❺ Reichstag (see pp. 62–63) All visitors to the Reichstag must register in advance. Instead of wasting precious time doing this on the day, prebook your tickets online ahead of your trip, choosing a time slot to tie in with your itinerary. If you arrive early, the ■ Bundeskanzleramt (Federal Chancellery; see p. 37) is an additional architectural highlight of Berlin's Government Quarter. For a great view of the whole quarter, cross Kanzlerbrücke (the bridge that crosses the Spree River behind the Bundeskanzleramt) to ■ Kanzlergarten. North of the Reichstag building, ■ Spreebogenpark (see p. 104) hugs the bend of the Spree River, providing pleasant waterfront strolling.

WHIRLWIND TOURS

Berlin in a Weekend

Explore the city's cultural highlights with this full-on tour of central Berlin.

❶ Hackesche Höfe (see pp. 80–81) **With its eight interconnected courtyards, this elegant art nouveau development is a haven of trendy cafés and boutiques. Walk south on Neue Promenade and then Burgstrasse.**

WHIRLWIND TOURS

❷ Berliner Dom (see p. 76) **Find your bearings in central Berlin from the top of the city's immense cathedral. Stroll through the Lustgarten and on to Museumsinsel.**

❸ Museumsinsel (see pp. 74–75) **Select a few highlights at the five museums on offer. Head west on Bodestrasse, then south on Oberwallstrasse to Französische Strasse.**

❹ Gendarmenmarkt (see pp. 60–61) **Visit the two churches on this handsome square. Exit on Kronenstrasse and walk west to Friedrichstrasse.**

Map labels:

KAPELLE-UFER
Bundestag
PLATZ DER REPUBLIK — Reichstag
SCHEIDEMANNSTR. — REGIERUNGS VIERTEL
Brandenburger Tor — PARISER PLATZ — Brandenburger Tor
TIERGARTEN
Holocaust Monument
OLD REGIERUNGS VIERTEL
VOSSSTRASSE
TIERGARTENTUNNEL
LENNÉSTR.
Sony Center
LEIPZIGER PLATZ
KULTUR FORUM — **Potsdamer Platz** ❻ — Potsdamer Platz
POTSDAMER STR.
Daimler Contemporary — Potsdamer Platz
MARLENE-DIETRICH-PLATZ
LINKSTRASSE
TILLA-DURIEUX-PARK
KÖTHENER STR.
STRESEMANN
Topographie des Terrors
ASKANISCHER PLATZ
Mendelssohn-Bartholdy-Park
MENDELSSOHN-BARTHOLDY-PARK — Anhalter Bahnhof
Möckernbrücke

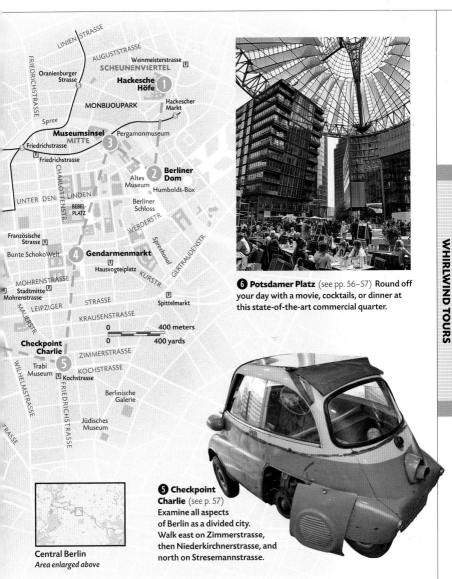

Map labels (Central Berlin):

LINIEN STRASSE

AUGUSTSTRASSE

Weinmeisterstrasse Ⓤ

SCHEUNENVIERTEL

FRIEDRICHSTRASSE

Oranienburger Strasse

Hackesche Höfe ❶

MONBIJOUPARK

Hackescher Markt

Spree

Museumsinsel ❸

MITTE

Pergamonmuseum

Friedrichstrasse Ⓤ

Friedrichstrasse

CHARLOTTENSTR.

Altes Museum

❷ **Berliner Dom**

Humboldt-Box

UNTER DEN LINDEN

BEBEL-PLATZ

Berliner Schloss

WERDERSTR.

Spreekanal

GERTRAUDENSTR.

Französische Strasse Ⓤ

Bunte SchokoWelt

❹ **Gendarmenmarkt**

Ⓤ Hausvogteiplatz

KURSTR.

MOHRENSTRASSE

Ⓤ Stadtmitte
Mohrenstrasse

MAUERSTR.

LEIPZIGER

STRASSE

KRAUSENSTRASSE

Ⓤ Spittelmarkt

0 ———— 400 meters

0 ———— 400 yards

Checkpoint Charlie

ZIMMERSTRASSE

Trabi Museum ❺ KOCHSTRASSE

Ⓤ Kochstrasse

WILHELMSTRASSE

FRIEDRICHSTRASSE

Berlinische Galerie

Jüdisches Museum

STRASSE

Central Berlin
Area enlarged above

❻ **Potsdamer Platz** (see pp. 56–57) Round off your day with a movie, cocktails, or dinner at this state-of-the-art commercial quarter.

❺ **Checkpoint Charlie** (see p. 57) Examine all aspects of Berlin as a divided city. Walk east on Zimmerstrasse, then Niederkirchnerstrasse, and north on Stresemannstrasse.

Tips

This second day of your weekend tour covers the best of Berlin's cultural highlights. Follow the cross-references for detailed information on each. Use these tips for shortcuts when visiting on limited time. There are also suggestions for additional sights nearby and places to eat and drink along the way.

WHIRLWIND TOURS

❶ **Hackesche Höfe** (see pp. 80–81) There's always a buzz of anticipation and excitement as the courtyard cafés and boutiques wake to a new day. Stop for coffee at the ■ Hackescher Hof Restaurant *(Hof 1, open from 7 a.m.),* then treat yourself to a hip souvenir.

❷ **Berliner Dom** (see p. 76) Before visiting Berlin's grand cathedral, step

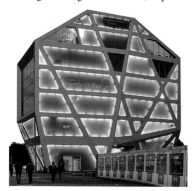

The façade of the Humboldt-Box is in stark contrast to the buildings of Museumsinsel.

into the futuristic ■ Humboldt-Box *(Schlossplatz 5)* to see a scale model of the reconstruction of the ■ Berliner Schloss (Royal Palace; see p. 119) currently underway at the southern end of Museumsinsel. Make your way to the ■ Humboldt Terrassen café/bar on the sixth floor, which has seating inside and out and fantastic views of the island. Skip the detailed tour of the cathedral if you are short of time, but do climb to the top of its dome for one of the more intimate views of central Berlin. Before moving on, take a break in the pretty gardens— the ■ Lustgarten (see p. 76)—opposite the cathedral's main entrance.

❸ **Museumsinsel** (see pp. 74–75, 82–85) Instead of trying to see all five museums in detail, pick one or two highlights from a couple— the Miletus and Ishtar Gates at the ■ Pergamonmuseum (see pp. 74–75), for example, or the ancient Greek statue known as the "Berlin Goddess" at the ■ Altes Museum (see p. 75). You'll make huge savings on ticket prices (and avoid waiting in line) if you buy one of several combined tickets available (see p. 75).

❹ **Gendarmenmarkt** (see pp. 60–61) This historic square is surrounded by shops and cafés. It is a great place to soak up the atmosphere of the city or to indulge in some retail therapy. Those with a sweet tooth can visit Ritter Sport's ■ Bunte SchokoWelt (World of Chocolate; see p. 41), where you can make your own chocolate bars. Or stop in at the largest chocolatier in Europe, ■ Fassbender & Rausch (*Charlottenstrasse 60*), in the square's southwestern corner. In December, the square hosts one of Berlin's atmospheric ■ Christmas markets (see pp. 120–121).

❺ **Checkpoint Charlie** (see p. 57) Take a detour past the ■ Topographie des Terrors (*Niederkirchnerstrasse 8*), the former Gestapo headquarters. Close to Checkpoint Charlie, the ■ Trabi Museum (see pp. 28–29) celebrates the state vehicle of the former GDR (DDR).

❻ **Potsdamer Platz** (see pp. 56–57) History buffs can inspect the remains of the ■ Berlin Wall and the outdoor exhibitions explaining how the

CUSTOMIZING **YOUR DAY**

Instead of jostling with tourists at Checkpoint Charlie, seek out some retail therapy. Glamorous Friedrichstrasse exudes an alluring, NYC-style vibe, thanks to its mix or upscale offices, restaurants, and exclusive retail outlets. Department stores **Galeries Lafayette** (*Nos. 76–78*) and **Quartier 206** (*No. 71*) offer high-end design and fashion goods, while the enormous bookstore **Dussmann** (*No. 90*) has a very good English selection on the ground floor.

square was once a wasteland, while shopaholics will find many great stores at the ■ Potsdamer Platz Arkaden (*Alte Potsdamer Strasse 7*). For something cultural, head to the nearby ■ Kulturforum (see Neue Nationalgalerie and Bauhaus-Archiv; pp. 96–97) or drop in at ■ Daimler Contemporary (*Alte Potsdamer Strasse 5*), which hosts almost 2,000 artworks—mostly from the 20th century—including several large sculptures. For sustenance, ■ Weilands Wellfood (*Marlene-Dietrich-Platz 1*) serves fresh, high-vitamin, low-calorie dishes in a bright and breezy canteen, while ■ Mommseneck (*Alte Potsdamer Strasse 1*) is the place to sample a range of international beers alongside traditional German dishes.

WHIRLWIND TOURS

Berlin for Fun

This east by west city tour combines skyline views and a Trabi Safari with some of the best classical music in Europe.

❻ Berliner Philharmonie (see p. 29) Round off your day with a concert in one of Europe's finest music venues at the heart of Berlin's Kulturforum.

❺ Deutsche Kinemathek (see p. 29) Explore Germany's fascinating cinematic history in this modern museum. Walk west on Potsdamer Strasse, then north on Scharounstrasse.

❹ Tiergarten (see pp. 29, 98–99) Take a rowboat out on the Neuer See or climb the victory column in Berlin's sprawling park. Continue east on Tiergartenstrasse.

BERLIN FOR FUN DISTANCE: 6.2 MILES (10 KM)
TIME: 11–12 HOURS S-BAHN/U-BAHN START: ALEXANDERPLATZ

1 Fernsehturm (see pp. 28, 77) Ascend to the dizzy heights of this socialist TV Tower for the best inner-city views of Berlin. Head north to Karl-Liebknecht-Strasse and follow Dircksenstrasse west to An der Spandauer Brücke. Take a right, and you'll soon hit Rosenthaler Strasse.

0   400 meters
0   400 yards

DOROTHEENSTÄDTISCHER FRIEDHOF
TORSTRASSE
LUISENSTRASSE
FRIEDRICHSTRASSE
AUGUSTSTRASSE
SCHEUNENVIERTEL
Oranienburger Strasse
Weinmeisterstrasse
MÜNZSTRASSE
KARL-LIEBKNECHTSTR.
WADZECKSTR.
REINHARDTSTR.
Hackesche Höfe **2**
MONBIJOUPARK
MITTE
Hackescher Markt
ALEXANDER-PLATZ
Alexanderplatz
Friedrichstrasse
Friedrichstrasse
Museumsinsel (Museum Island)
Fernsehturm 1
Berliner Dom
REICHSTAGUFER
CHARLOTTENSTR.
Deutsches Historisches Museum
NIKOLAIVIERTEL
REGIERUNGS-VIERTEL
PARISER PLATZ
UNTER DEN LINDEN
BEBEL-PLATZ
PRINZESSINNEN-GARTEN
Brandenburger Tor
BEHRENSTR.
Französische Strasse
FRANZÖSISCHE STR.
WERDERSTR.
Spree
HOLOCAUST MONUMENT
GLINKASTR.
GENDARMENMARKT
Hausvogteiplatz
OLD REGIERUNGS-VIERTEL
Stadtmitte
Mohrenstrasse
LEIPZIGER STRASSE
Potsdamer Platz
Trabi Museum
Checkpoint Charlie
3
Kochstrasse

Central Berlin
Area enlarged above

2 Hackesche Höfe (see pp. 28, 80–81) Have a splurge on boutique treats. Return to Karl-Liebknecht-Strasse for a bus (M48) heading south at the intersection with Spandauer Strasse. Alight at Friedrichstrasse.

3 Trabi Museum (see pp. 28–29) Indulge in a little "Ostalgie," then hit the streets on a Trabi Safari. Take the U-Bahn (U6) to Friedrichstrasse, then the S-Bahn (S5 or S7) to Tiergarten.

WHIRLWIND TOURS

WHIRLWIND TOURS

Fernsehturm

1 Berlin's TV Tower was once a major symbol of socialist East Germany. Today, its slim, tall form is present on everything from postcards and buttons to T-shirts. Take the elevator up to the space-age ball at the top for views of the city's major sights—the **Reichstag** (see pp. 62–63), **Brandenburger Tor** (see p. 54), and **Potsdamer Platz** (see pp. 56–57). You can even see the monumental **Olympiastadion** (see pp. 158–159) from here.

Panoramastrasse 1A • www.tv-turm.de • 030 24 75 75 87 5 • €€€ • S-Bahn/U-Bahn: Alexanderplatz

Hackesche Höfe

2 These eight lavishly restored courtyards have become one of central Berlin's most attractive shopping destinations. Originally opened in 1906 to house factories and offices, the courtyards now brim with boutiques and cultural venues. Scattered throughout, clothing boutiques include **Lisa D** (*Hof 5, 030 28 34 35 4*), **Jordan** (*Hof 8, 030 28 15 04 3*), and **Avalon** (*Hof 8, 030 61 51 85 6*). For souvenirs with a distinctly German twist, head to **Ampelmann** (*Hof 5, 030 44 72 64 38*), for an incredible range of goods related to the famed East German traffic-light man.

Rosenthaler Strasse 40–1 • S-Bahn: Hackescher Markt

Join other Trabant enthusiasts on the Trabi Museum's fun safari.

Trabi Museum

3 This relatively new enterprise at the Checkpoint Charlie site pays homage to the "Volkswagen of the East" in an exhibition that combines a straight history of the Trabant with a little "Ostalgie"—a play on the German words for East (*Ost*) and nostalgia (*Nostalgie*). In the former GDR (DDR), years used to pass between ordering a Trabant and actually taking delivery.

Today, you can get behind the wheel of a Trabant yourself and join a Trabi Safari *(from €30)* through the streets of Berlin. You'll need your driver's license and, although you can turn up on the day, it is a good idea to book online in advance (see website for details).

Zimmerstrasse 14–15 • www.trabi-museum.com • 030 30 20 10 30 • €€
• U-Bahn: Kochstrasse

Tiergarten

4 If you're visiting the park at dusk, a magical sight awaits you at the **Gaslaternen-Freilichtmuseum** (Gas Lantern Museum; *Joseph-Haydn-Strasse, 030 90 25 41 24)*, whose outdoor exhibition displays 90 historic gas lanterns from different parts of Berlin. Beautifully restored, they illuminate a winding path from dusk. If visiting in summer, head to **Neuer See** for a row on the lake. Both the museum and the lake are close to Tiergarten S-Bahn station.

Strasse des 17. Juni • S-Bahn: Tiergarten

Deutsche Kinemathek

5 The entertaining and modern multimedia Film and Television Museum is a must for cinema buffs. Spanning Germany's entire filmmaking history, there are posters and photos, film costumes, scripts, and original props. Watch for dedicated sections on stars such as Marlene Dietrich and *Metropolis* director Fritz Lang.

Potsdamer Strasse 2 • www.deutsche-kinemathek.de • 030 30 09 03 0 • €€ • Closed Mon. • S-Bahn: Potsdamer Platz

Berliner Philharmonie

6 Book tickets in advance for Berlin's Philharmonic Orchestra—either in the **Grosser Saal** (Great Hall) or the **Kammermusiksaal** (Chamber Music Hall). If visiting in September, check out the program for the **Musikfest Berlin** music festival.

Herbert-von-Karajan-Strasse 1 • www.berliner-philharmoniker.de • 030 25 48 80
• €€–€€€€€ • S-Bahn: Potsdamer Platz

Berlin for Spies

Follow this spy trail through Berlin's totalitarian east—the hub of European espionage during the Cold War years.

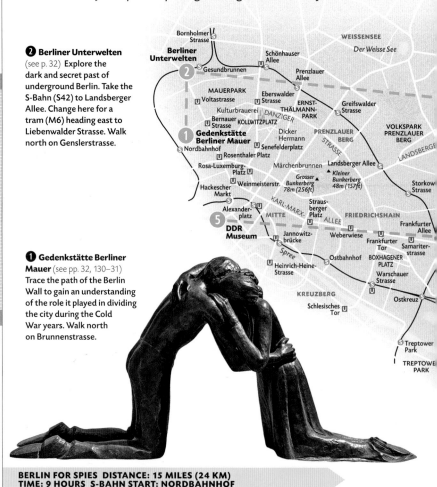

WHIRLWIND TOURS

❷ Berliner Unterwelten (see p. 32) **Explore the dark and secret past of underground Berlin. Take the S-Bahn (S42) to Landsberger Allee. Change here for a tram (M6) heading east to Liebenwalder Strasse. Walk north on Genslerstrasse.**

❶ Gedenkstätte Berliner Mauer (see pp. 32, 130–31) **Trace the path of the Berlin Wall to gain an understanding of the role it played in dividing the city during the Cold War years. Walk north on Brunnenstrasse.**

Bornholmer Strasse

WEISSENSEE

Der Weisse See

Berliner Unterwelten

❷ Gesundbrunnen

Schönhauser Allee

Prenzlauer Allee

MAUERPARK
Voltastrasse
Eberswalder Strasse
Kulturbrauerei DANZIGER
Bernauer KOLLWITZPLATZ
Strasse

ERNST-THÄLMANN-PARK

Greifswalder Strasse

❶ **Gedenkstätte Berliner Mauer**

Dicker Hermann

PRENZLAUER BERG

VOLKSPARK PRENZLAUER BERG

Nordbahnhof

Senefelderplatz

Rosa-Luxemburg-Platz
Rosenthaler Platz

Märchenbrunnen

Landsberger Allee

LANDSBERGE

Hackescher Markt
Weinmeisterstr.
Grosser Bunkerberg 78m (256ft)
▲ Kleiner Bunkerberg 48m (157ft)

Storkow Strasse

Alexander-platz

KARL-MARX-

Straus-berger Platz

FRIEDRICHSHAIN

Frankfurter Allee

❺ **DDR Museum**

MITTE

ALLEE

Jannowitz-brücke

Weberwiese

Frankfurter Tor

Samariter-strasse

Spree

Ostbahnhof

BOXHAGENER PLATZ

Heinrich-Heine-Strasse

Warschauer Strasse

KREUZBERG

Schlesisches Tor

Ostkreuz

Treptower Park

TREPTOWE PARK

**BERLIN FOR SPIES DISTANCE: 15 MILES (24 KM)
TIME: 9 HOURS S-BAHN START: NORDBAHNHOF**

❸ Gedenkstätte Hohenschönhausen (see p. 32)
Hear stories from past inmates at this former Stasi prison. Return to Liebenwalder Strasse. Catch a bus (256) south to Frankfurter Allee and walk west.

❹ Stasi-Museum (see p. 33)
Take a tour of House 1—the former headquarters of the Ministry of State Security. Take the U-Bahn (U5) from Magdalenenstrasse to Alexanderplatz and cross the square.

❺ DDR Museum
(see p. 33) **Experience life as it was for civilians under the former Soviet regime.**

East Berlin
Area enlarged above

IN **THE KNOW**

Opposite the Visitor
Center at the Gedenkstätte
Berliner Mauer stands
Nordbahnhof station,
home to an exhibition on
the Ghost Stations of the
GDR (DDR) years. These
stations were closed during
the division, despite being
on functioning East–
West lines, because they
represented a risk of escape.
Stop by to read stories of
would-be escapees who fell
prey to Stasi booby traps
and tales of the few who
succeeded in fleeing.

Gedenkstätte Berliner Mauer

1 The Berlin Wall Memorial stretches the length of Bernauer Strasse. Drop into the **Visitor Center** for exhibitions relating to the memorial and an overview of its features. Listen to recorded accounts at each stage and discover the fates of those who lost their lives trying to escape here. Ascend to a viewing platform that overlooks a stretch of the Death Strip as it was when manned by guards in watchtowers.

Bernauer Strasse 111 / 119 • www.berliner-mauer
-gedenkstaette.de • 030 46 79 86 66 6 • Visitor Center
closed Mon. and Dec. 24–25 • S-Bahn: Nordbahnhof

Berliner Unterwelten

2 Walk beneath the city streets with Berlin Underworlds, an organization operating a range of exploratory tours from a bunker at Gesundbrunnen S-Bahn station. Tour 1 (*11 a.m., days often vary by season; no reservations, no credit cards*), explores one of the few remaining underground bunkers, as it was left after World War II. Check the website for tour requirements ahead of your trip.

Brunnenstrasse 105 • www.berliner-unterwelten.de • 030 49 91 05 17 • €€€
• Closed Jan. 1, Dec. 22–25 • S-Bahn: Gesundbrunnen

Gedenkstätte Hohenschönhausen

3 With interiors that remain much as they were when this sinister institution was in its heyday, the Hohenschönhausen Memorial offers insight into prison life under the Soviet regime. To take a tour of the prison—they are often led by former inmates—plan your visit to coincide with an English-language tour (*Wed., Sat., and Sun., 2:30 p.m.; no reservation needed, but arrive by 2:15 p.m.*).

Genslerstrasse 66 • www.stiftung-hsh.de • 030 98 60 82 30 • €€ • Closed Jan. 1,
Dec. 24–26, and 31 • Bus: 256 (Liebenwalder Strasse)

Stasi-Museum

4 Housed in the former headquarters of the Ministry of State Security, this museum relates the chilling story of how one half of the population spied on the other. Seek out the intriguing displays of the gadgetry that underpinned their surveillance activities.

Ruschestrasse 103 • www.stasimuseum.de • 030 55 36 85 4 • €€ • U-Bahn: Magdalenenstrasse

DDR Museum

5 Discover the truth about life for ordinary civilians, breathe in the original aroma of an East German living room, and pick up the phone (which you'll find has been bugged). If you think you're tough enough, take on the challenge of a Stasi interrogation.

Karl-Liebknecht-Strasse 1 • www.ddr-museum.de • 030 84 71 23 73 1 • €€ • S-Bahn: Hackescher Markt

Look closely to see doors hidden in this photographic wall. They open to reveal Stasi secrets.

4 DZ Bank Building (see pp. 36–37) Marvel at Frank Gehry's remarkable atrium with its split-level spaces, curving glass ceilings, and extraordinary conference room. Walk north on Ebertstrasse.

5 Reichstag (see pp. 37, 62–63) Admire Sir Norman Foster's huge glass dome, one of the most symbolic structures of the post-wall era. Walk east on Scheidemannstrasse, then north on Heinrich-von-Gagern-Strasse.

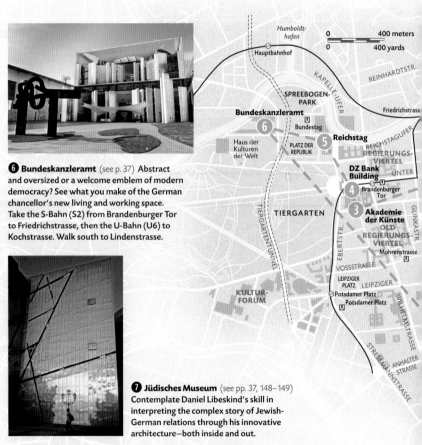

6 Bundeskanzleramt (see p. 37) Abstract and oversized or a welcome emblem of modern democracy? See what you make of the German chancellor's new living and working space. Take the S-Bahn (S2) from Brandenburger Tor to Friedrichstrasse, then the U-Bahn (U6) to Kochstrasse. Walk south to Lindenstrasse.

7 Jüdisches Museum (see pp. 37, 148–149) Contemplate Daniel Libeskind's skill in interpreting the complex story of Jewish-German relations through his innovative architecture—both inside and out.

BERLIN FOR ARCHITECTURE FANS DISTANCE: 5 MILES (8 KM) TIME: 8 HOURS S-BAHN START: HACKESCHER MARKT

Berlin for Contemporary Architecture Fans

See how the crème de la crème of contemporary architects has changed the face of Berlin since the fall of the Berlin Wall.

① Neues Museum (see pp. 36, 82–85) Discover why people waited in line for six hours to see the internal restoration of this museum *before* it was filled with exhibits. Walk through Lustgarten and cross the Spree River onto Unter den Linden.

③ Akademie der Künste (see p. 36) Step beyond the glass facade at the Academy of Arts to discover an interior by Günter Behnisch with a spectacularly expressionistic twist. Head next door.

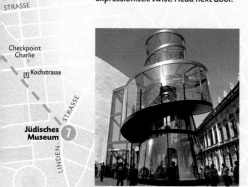

② Deutsches Historisches Museum (see pp. 36, 60) Consider I. M. Pei's success in rising to the challenge of designing a contemporary annex for the most prominent baroque building on Unter den Linden.
Continue west to Pariser Platz.

Central Berlin
Area enlarged above

Neues Museum

1 David Chipperfield's sophisticated 2005 restoration of the New Museum makes no attempt to hide the extensive damage sustained during World War II. You'll see intricately restored murals and bullet-strafed walls juxtaposed with assertive new spaces and solid oak doors that could pass as part of the original building.

Bodestrasse 1–3 • www.neues-museum.de • 030 20 90 51 01 • €€€ • Closed Dec. 24 • S-Bahn: Hackescher Markt

Deutsches Historisches Museum

2 I. M. Pei's sleek glass-and-limestone extension of the German Historical Museum contrasts strongly with the heavily decorated baroque Zeughaus (armory) next door. Yet see how it defers to the older building through the transparency of its vast glazed atrium lobby.

Unter den Linden 2 • www.dhm.de • 030 20 30 44 44 • €€ • Closed Dec. 24 • U-Bahn: Französische Strasse

Akademie der Künste

3 What little survived World War II is now encased in a transparent structure of cascading steel-and-glass components that somehow contain an archive, an auditorium, offices, a café, and a reception room. As you consider this remarkable interior, you'll appreciate that it is no mean feat of structural engineering.

Pariser Platz 4 • www.adk.de • 030 20 05 71 00 0 • € • U-Bahn: Brandenburger Tor

Curving glass ceilings separate the floors of DZ Bank's complex, multistoried foyer.

DZ Bank Building

4 Frank Gehry's sober sandstone-and-glass facade hides the organic exuberance of his interior, which features an enormous horse-head-shaped, zinc-clad conference room jutting into the atrium and a steel-and-glass floor that allows you to look into the restaurant below.

Pariser Platz 3 • www.dzbank.de • 030 20 24 10 • U-Bahn: Brandenburger Tor

Reichstag

5 Norman Foster's 1999 renovation of the originally neoclassical national parliamentary building is punctuated with accents of war damage and Russian graffiti and crowned by the much talked about glass dome. The high-tech design is also superefficient, fueled by vegetable oil, geothermal energy, and the sun.

Platz der Republik 1 • www.bundestag.de • 030 22 73 21 52 • Closed Dec. 24 • U-Bahn: Brandenburger Tor

Bundeskanzleramt

6 Inspired by such disparate works as the mosques of Isfahan and the buildings of American architect Louis Kahn, the new white Chancellery is a focal point of a much larger scheme designed by local architects Axel Schultes and Charlotte Frank. They have created what they call a "Federal Ribbon"—an east-by-west corridor of new government buildings that crosses the Spree River twice at former Cold War boundaries, thereby symbolically reconnecting the city.

Willy-Brandt-Strasse 1 • 030 18 27 22 72 0 • U-Bahn: Bundestag

Jüdisches Museum

7 A crucial contribution to Jewish-German understanding and reconciliation in the wake of the horrors of the 20th century, Daniel Libeskind's lightning-bolt floorplan combines with slashed windows, zinc cladding, concrete voids, and symbol-laden landscapes. This masterpiece of 21st-century architecture remains one of the most radical buildings in Europe today.

Lindenstrasse 9–14 • www.jmberlin.de • 030 25 99 33 00 • €€ • Closed Rosh Hashanah, Yom Kippur, and Dec. 24 • U-Bahn: Kochstrasse

Berlin in a Weekend with Kids

*A fun-packed day with sea creatures to stroke, buttons to push,
and chocolate—not only to eat, but to make as well.*

❶ Sea Life Center (see p. 40)
Visit the AquaDom in this exciting
underwater world. Walk south on
Spandauer Strasse, then west on
Karl-Liebknecht-Strasse.

❷ DDR Museum (see p. 40) Enjoy
some push-button fun at one of the
city's most interactive museums.
Continue south on Spandauer
Strasse, then east on Grunerstrasse.

❸ Loxx Miniaturwelten (see p. 40) Sightsee
this miniature city within the city. Step into
Alexanderplatz and head straight for the
space-age Fernsehturm.

**BERLIN WITH KIDS, DAY 1 DISTANCE: 3 MILES (5 KM)
TIME: 7 HOURS S-BAHN START: HACKESCHER MARKT**

Sidebar: WHIRLWIND TOURS

❹ Fernsehturm (see pp. 41, 77) Take in the spectacular views from Berlin's tallest building. Hop on the S-Bahn (S7) at Alexanderplatz and change to the U-Bahn (U6) at Friedrichstrasse. Alight at Französische Strasse.

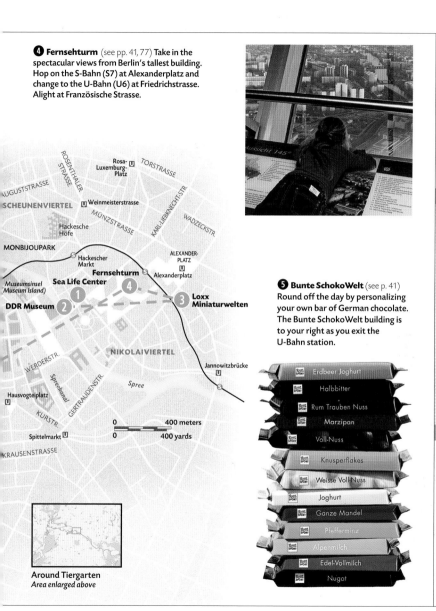

❺ Bunte SchokoWelt (see p. 41) Round off the day by personalizing your own bar of German chocolate. The Bunte SchokoWelt building is to your right as you exit the U-Bahn station.

Around Tiergarten
Area enlarged above

Erdbeer Joghurt
Halbbitter
Rum Trauben Nuss
Marzipan
Voll-Nuss
Knusperflakes
Weisse Voll Nuss
Joghurt
Ganze Mandel
Pfefferminz
Alpenmilch
Edel-Vollmilch
Nugat

Sea Life Center

1 Indulge your kids in some fishy fun in this vibrant underwater world. Head straight for the **Interactive Rockpool,** with its sea stars, crabs, and sea anemones, some of which may be touched. The real highlight comes in the shape of the 80-foot-tall (24 m) **AquaDom**—the largest cylindrical fish tank in the world—complete with a coral reef and 100 species of beautiful, exotic fish that include triggerfish, blowfish, and silver moonfish. Book online to get up to 40 percent discounts.

Spandauer Strasse 3 • www.visitsealife.com • 030 99 28 00 • €€€€ • Closed Dec. 24 • S-Bahn: Hackescher Markt

SAVVY **TRAVELER**

Check the Sea Life Center website in advance to see if you can plan your visit to coincide with one of the many daily feeding times.

DDR Museum

2 Step into the former German Democratic Republic at this hands-on and fun museum. Kids can sit behind the wheel of a Trabant, the iconic East German car—they can even turn on the ignition. See what's cooking in the authentic East Berlin kitchen and watch the kids play at being spies with hidden Stasi microphones. There are endless drawers and doors to open throughout, each one providing a new insight into this very different world.

Karl-Liebknecht-Strasse 1 • www.ddr-museum.de • 030 84 71 23 73 1 • €€ • S-Bahn: Hackescher Markt

Loxx Miniaturwelten

3 See if your kids can pick out the city sights in this 1:87 scale model of Berlin, complete with 2.5 miles (4 km) of railroad, 400 model trains, 10,000 vehicles, and 50,000 tiny inhabitants going about their daily business. Not only do children have fun spotting all the major landmarks, they love the attention to detail that extends to factories, apartment blocks, and a model airport with Boeing 747s taking off through makeshift clouds of cotton wool.

4th Floor, Alexa Mall, Grunerstrasse 20 • www.loxx-berlin.de • 030 44 72 30 22 • €€€ • S-Bahn/U-Bahn: Alexanderplatz

Fernsehturm

4 Berlin's rocket-shaped TV Tower is a major draw for kids. Not only does a high-speed elevator whisk them up 650 feet (200 m) in just 40 seconds, but there's a rotating restaurant at the top (the **Sphere;** *030 24 75 75 87 5, €€–€€€*). Purchase a VIP ticket online ahead of your trip, and you can reserve a specific time to visit.

Panoramastrasse 1A • www.tv-turm.de • 030 24 75 75 87 5 • €€€ • S-Bahn: Alexanderplatz

Bunte SchokoWelt

5 Ritter Sport's colorful flagship store features a **History and Making of Chocolate** exhibit where kids can learn all about Germany's best known chocolate brand. There is also a café serving to-die-for hot chocolate. Best of all, kids can design their own candy bars and watch them being made. Make a reservation in advance.

Französische Strasse 24 • www.ritter-sport.de • 030 20 09 50 80 • U-Bahn: Französische Strasse

WHIRLWIND TOURS

Kids have everything on hand for making Ritter Sport chocolate bars of their own.

Berlin in a Weekend with Kids

*Today's tour is one big adventure that sees kids playing
with gadgets and gizmos and scaring themselves silly.*

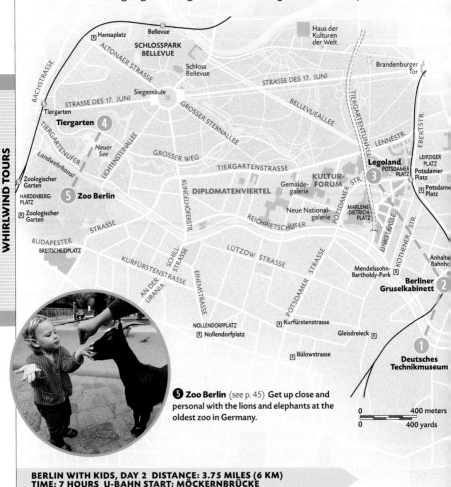

WHIRLWIND TOURS

Hansaplatz

Bellevue

SCHLOSSPARK
BELLEVUE

Haus der
Kulturen
der Welt

ALTONAER STRASSE

Schloss
Bellevue

Brandenburger
Tor

BACHSTRASSE

STRASSE DES 17. JUNI

STRASSE DES 17. JUNI

Siegessäule

BELLEVUEALLEE

EBERTSTR.

Tiergarten

Tiergarten ④

GROSSER STERNALLEE

TIERGARTENTUNNEL

LENNÉSTR.

LEIPZIGER
PLATZ

Legoland ③

Potsdamer
Platz

TIERGARTENUFER

Neuer
See

LICHTENSTEINALLEE

GROSSER WEG

TIERGARTENSTRASSE

POTSDAMER STR.

POTSDAMER
PLATZ

Landwehrkanal

Zoologischer
Garten

**KULTUR-
FORUM**

Potsdamer
Platz

HARDENBERG-
PLATZ

⑤ **Zoo Berlin**

KLINGELHÖFERSTR.

DIPLOMATENVIERTEL

Gemälde-
galerie

MARLENE-
DIETRICH-
PLATZ

Zoologischer
Garten

Neue National-
galerie

REICHPIETSCHUFER

LINKSTRASSE

KÖTHENER STR.

STRASSE

Anhalter
Bahnhof

BUDAPESTER

BREITSCHEIDPLATZ

LÜTZOW STRASSE

POTSDAMER STRASSE

KURFÜRSTENSTRASSE

SCHILL STRASSE

Mendelssohn-
Bartholdy-Park

**Berliner
Gruselkabinett** ②

AN DER URANIA

EINEMSTRASSE

NOLLENDORFPLATZ

Kurfürstenstrasse

Nollendorfplatz

Gleisdreieck

①
**Deutsches
Technikmuseum**

Bülowstrasse

⑤ **Zoo Berlin** (see p. 45) **Get up close and
personal with the lions and elephants at the
oldest zoo in Germany.**

0 ————— 400 meters
0 ————— 400 yards

**BERLIN WITH KIDS, DAY 2 DISTANCE: 3.75 MILES (6 KM)
TIME: 7 HOURS U-BAHN START: MÖCKERNBRÜCKE**

❶ Deutsches Technikmuseum
(see p. 44) Watch your kids have fun coming to grips with technology. Walk north along the Spree (Tempelhofer Ufer), crossing the bridge on Schöneberger Ufer.

❷ Berliner Gruselkabinett
(see pp. 44–45) Three floors of fun and horror in a World-War-II-era bunker. Take the S-Bahn (S) from Anhalter Bahnhof to Potsdamer Platz. Walk east on Potsdamer Strasse.

❸ Legoland (see p. 45) You'll see the giant Lego giraffe as you approach this mini-brick haven. Take the S-Bahn (S 2) from Potsdamer Platz to Tiergarten.

❹ Tiergarten (see pp. 45, 98–99)
Enjoy the myriad pleasures and playgrounds of Berlin's royal park. Wend your way to the park's southwest corner and on to Hardenbergplatz.

Around Tiergarten
Area enlarged above

ANHALTER STRASSE

STRESEMANNSTRASSE

Möckernbrücke

Deutsches Technikmuseum

1 Extensive coverage of all things technological awaits the curious child at the German Museum of Technology. Instead of trying to see everything, focus on just one or two of the 14 permanent exhibitions on offer, from transportation and computer science to paper technology and textile work. Kids can learn how just about everything gets made—from medicines to suitcases—and there are interactive exhibits throughout.

Trebbiner Strasse 9 • www.sdtb.de • 030 902540 • €€ • Closed Mon.
• U-Bahn: Möckernbrücke

Berliner Gruselkabinett

2 Housed within a real World War II bunker, the Cabinet of Horrors is the ultimate treat for kids who delight in the macabre. Start in the gloomy basement for grisly tales of war or make

Life-size planes, trains, ships, and lots, lots more at the German Museum of Technology

straight for the second-floor demos of gruesome medical treatments. Whatever you do, don't miss the house of horrors on the third floor with its pitch-black maze, costumed actors who jump out of the darkness, and the bloodcurdling screams of your petrified children.

Schöneberger Strasse 23a • www.gruselkabinett-berlin.de • 030 26 55 55 46 • €€€ • S-Bahn: Anhalter Bahnhof

Legoland

3 The imagination knows no bounds when it comes to one of the world's best-selling toys. Kids journey through a network of rooms with tubs of colorful bricks for rummaging, a roller coaster, and a factory in which they can help turn hot plastic into Lego bricks.

Potsdamer Strasse 4 • www.legolanddiscoverycentre.de • 030 30 10 40 0 • €€€€ • S-Bahn: Potsdamer Platz

Tiergarten

4 Berlin's largest park has endless opportunities for kids: playgrounds, forested areas, lakes, and meadows. The largest play area is on John-Foster-Dulles-Allee and features a sandbox, tire swings, and a climbing net. It's a good 20-minute walk from the S-Bahn station, but well worth it—take a picnic for sustenance.

Strasse des 17. Juni • S-Bahn: Tiergarten

Zoo Berlin

5 The oldest (1844) animal park in Germany boasts 1,570 species—more than any other zoo in Europe. Plan your trip to coincide with feeding time for the monkeys (*4 p.m.*)—a riotous affair.

Hardenbergplatz 8 • www.zoo-berlin.de • 030 25 40 10 • €€€€–€€€€€ • S-Bahn: Tiergarten

GOOD **EATS**

■ **ANDY'S DINER & BAR**
This all-American diner serves U.S. classics from spare ribs to burgers. Special deals are available from the lunchtime menu. **Potsdamer Strasse 1, 030 23 00 49 90, €€**

■ **GALERIES LAFAYETTE DELIKATESSEN**
There's something for everyone in this high-end French and Mediterranean deli—including almost 200 types of cheese, fresh baguettes, and savory pastries. Take-out or eat-in available. **Friedrichstrasse 76–78, 030 20 94 80, €€€**

WHIRLWIND TOURS

PART 2

Berlin's Neighborhoods

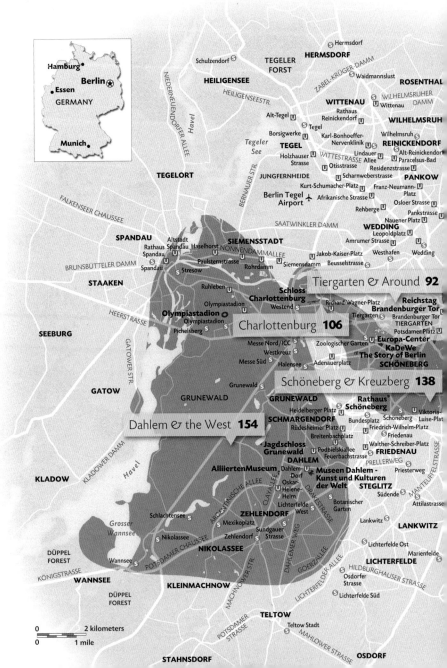

Hamburg•
Berlin ⊛
•Essen
GERMANY

Munich•

Hermsdorf Ⓢ

TEGELER
FORST

Schulzendorf Ⓢ

HERMSDORF

ZABEL-KRÜGER-DAMM

Waidmannslust Ⓢ

ROSENTHAL

HEILIGENSEE

WILHELMSRUHER
DAMM

HEILIGENSEESTR.

WITTENAU

Wittenau Ⓤ

NIEDERNEUENDORFER ALLEE

Alt-Tegel Ⓤ

Rathaus
Reinickendorf Ⓤ

WILHELMSRUH

Tegel Ⓢ

Borsigwerke Ⓤ

Karl-Bonhoeffer-
Nervenklinik Ⓤ

Wilhelmsruh Ⓢ

REINICKENDORF

Tegeler
See

TEGEL

Holzhauser
Strasse Ⓤ

WITTESTRASSE Allee Ⓤ

Lindauer Ⓤ
Allee

Alt-Reinickendorf Ⓢ
Paracelsus-Bad Ⓤ

TEGELORT

JUNGFERNHEIDE

Otisstrasse Ⓤ

Residenzstrasse Ⓤ

BERNAUER STR.

Scharnweberstrasse Ⓤ

PANKOW

FALKENSEER CHAUSSEE

Berlin Tegel ✈
Airport

Kurt-Schumacher-Platz Ⓤ

Afrikanische Strasse Ⓤ

Franz-Neumann-
Platz Ⓤ

Osloer Strasse Ⓤ

Rehberge Ⓤ

Pankstrasse Ⓤ

SAATWINKLER DAMM

Nauener Platz Ⓤ

WEDDING

Leopoldplatz Ⓤ

SPANDAU

Altstadt
Spandau

SIEMENSSTADT

Amrumer Strasse Ⓤ

Ⓤ Ⓢ

BRUNSBÜTTELER DAMM

Rathaus
Spandau Ⓤ

Haselhorst
Ⓤ

NONNENDAMMALLEE

Jakob-Kaiser-Platz Ⓤ

Westhafen Ⓢ

Wedding
Ⓢ

Spandau Ⓢ

Paulsternstrasse Ⓤ

Rohrdamm Ⓤ

Siemensdamm Ⓤ

Beusselstrasse Ⓢ

Stresow Ⓢ

STAAKEN

Ruhleben Ⓤ

Schloss
Charlottenburg

Tiergarten & Around 92

HEERSTRASSE

Olympiastadion Ⓢ

Westend Ⓢ

Richard-Wagner-Platz Ⓤ

Reichstag
Brandenburger Tor Ⓤ

SEEBURG

Olympiastadion Ⓤ
Olympiastadion ⊙

Tiergarten Ⓢ

Brandenburger Tor Ⓤ
TIERGARTEN

GATOWER STR.

Pichelsberg Ⓢ

Charlottenburg 106

Potsdamer Platz Ⓤ

Messe Nord/ICC Ⓢ

Zoologischer Garten Ⓢ

Ⓢ Ⓤ Europa-Center
★ KaDeWe
★ The Story of Berlin
SCHÖNEBERG

GATOW

Westkreuz Ⓤ

Messe Süd Ⓢ

Halensee Ⓢ

Adenauerplatz Ⓤ

Schöneberg & Kreuzberg 138

GRUNEWALD

Grunewald Ⓢ

GRUNEWALD

KLADOWER DAMM

Dahlem & the West 154

SCHMARGENDORF

Heidelberger Platz Ⓢ Ⓤ

Rüdesheimer Platz Ⓤ

Rathaus
Schöneberg Ⓤ

Bundesplatz Ⓢ

Ⓤ Viktoria-
Luise-Plat

Schöneberg Ⓢ

Friedrich-Wilhelm-Platz Ⓤ

Friedenau Ⓢ

KLADOW

Havel

Breitenbachplatz Ⓤ

Podbielskiallee Ⓤ

Walther-Schreiber-Platz Ⓤ
FRIEDENAU

Jagdschloss
Grunewald

Feuerbachstrasse Ⓢ

PRELLERWEG

Priesterweg Ⓢ

DAHLEM

AlliiertenMuseum

Dahlem-Ⓤ
Dorf

Museen Dahlem -
Kunst und Kulturen
der Welt

STEGLITZ

Grosser
Wannsee

Oskar-
Helene-
Heim Ⓤ

Lichterfelde Ⓢ
West

Botanischer
Garten Ⓢ

Südende Ⓢ

Attilastrasse Ⓢ

Schlachtensee Ⓢ

ZEHLENDORF

ARGENTINISCHE ALLEE

CLAYALLEE

Mexikoplatz Ⓢ

Lankwitz Ⓢ

LANKWITZ

Nikolassee Ⓢ

POTSDAMER CHAUSSEE

Zehlendorf Ⓢ

Sundgauer
Strasse Ⓢ

DAHLEMER WEG

DREISTRASSE

Lichterfelde Ost Ⓢ

Marienfelde Ⓢ

DÜPPEL
FOREST

NIKOLASSEE

Wannsee Ⓢ

LICHTERFELDE

KÖNIGSTRASSE

NACHTIGALLENSTR.

LICHTERFELDER ALLEE

GOERZALLEE

HILDBURGHAUSER STRASSE

Osdorfer
Strasse Ⓢ

WANNSEE

KLEINMACHNOW

Lichterfelde Süd Ⓢ

DÜPPEL
FOREST

POTSDAMER STRASSE

TELTOW

Teltow Stadt Ⓢ

MAHLOWER STRASSE

STAHNSDORF

OSDORF

0   2 kilometers
0   1 mile

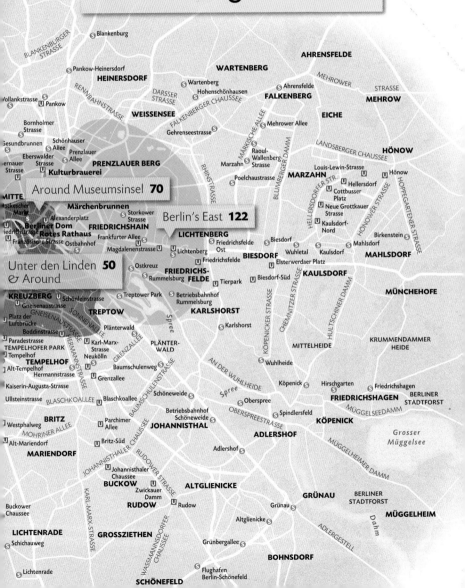

Unter den Linden & Around

Stroll the streets of this neighborhood and it is difficult to imagine that, during the Cold War years, the Brandenburger Tor (Brandenburg Gate) was stranded in wasteland with a near-derelict Reichstag close by. Stopping just short of the Berlin Wall, the city's historic boulevard, Unter den Linden, became all but redundant for almost 30 years. Today, however, these landmarks define a neighborhood that is every bit the epicenter of a vital European capital city—just as it was in the days of the Prussian Empire. While Unter den Linden and Gendarmenmarkt hark back to the 18th and 19th centuries, Checkpoint Charlie, Bebelplatz, and the Holocaust Monument are poignant reminders of a more recent past. And all the while, the soaring skyscrapers at Potsdamer Platz shimmer with a dynamism that screams 21st century.

◀ **The design for the Brandenburg Gate, Berlin's most famous monument, took inspiration from the entrance to the Acropolis in Athens.**

Unter den Linden & Around

From Prussian grandeur to Cold War nostalgia, the monuments of Berlin's historic center reveal the city's vibrant past.

1 Reichstag (see pp. 62–63) Start with breakfast at the Reichstag. Make your way to Scheidemannstrasse. Head east until you reach Ebertstrasse, where the Brandenburg Gate will come into view. Approach Pariser Platz from here.

2 Pariser Platz (see pp. 54) **Enter** this spacious square through the mighty Brandenburg Gate. On leaving, return to Ebertstrasse and walk south.

3 Holocaust Monument (see p. 55) Contemplate the fate of many Jews during the Nazi era at this sobering monument. Continue south on Ebertstrasse.

4 Potsdamer Platz (see pp. 56–57) **Marvel** at the ultramodern buildings of this once derelict square. Walk south on Stresemannstrasse, then turn onto Niederkirchnerstrasse, heading east.

**UNTER DEN LINDEN & AROUND   DISTANCE: 3.5 MILES (5.6 KM)
TIME: APPROX. 10 HOURS U-BAHN START: BRANDENBURGER TOR**

⑩ Gendarmenmarkt (see pp. 60–61) Wind up at lively Gendarmenmarkt, with its two 18th-century churches and striking concert hall.

⑨ Deutsches Historisches Museum (see p. 60) Select highlights from the 2,000 years of history on offer. Return to Bebelplatz and walk south to join Französische Strasse heading west.

⑧ Neue Wache (see p. 59) Drop in to see Käthe Kollwitz's stirring sculpture, before continuing east on Unter den Linden.

⑦ Bebelplatz (see p. 59) Seek out the low-key memorial at the center of this sedate square. Cross the road to reach Unter den Linden No. 4.

⑥ KunstHalle (see p. 58) Enjoy a tour of this minimalist art gallery hosting globally minded contemporary art exhibitions. Continue east on Unter den Linden.

⑤ Checkpoint Charlie (see p. 57) Follow the former Berlin Wall trail along Niederkirchnerstrasse to the site of the former Checkpoint Charlie and modern-day Wall Museum. Walk north on Friedrichstrasse to reach Unter den Linden.

The terrace café at Hotel Adlon on Pariser Platz is a major draw for tourists hoping to spot the odd celebrity.

Reichstag

See pp. 62–63.

Platz der Republik 1 • www.bundestag.de • 030 30 22 73 21 52 • Closed Dec. 24 • S-Bahn/U-Bahn: Brandenburger Tor

Pariser Platz

Approaching Pariser Platz from the west, you'll pass straight through the monumental **Brandenburger Tor** (Brandenburg Gate; *www.brandenburgertor.de, 030 25 00 23 33*). This gate symbolizes victory, peace, division, and unity all in one. Admire the sextet of Doric columns topped with the Quadriga, or Goddess of Victory, before strolling through the gate and into Pariser Platz. The meticulously restored buildings that flank this elegant square include the British, French, and U.S. embassies. For art lovers, **Max Liebermann Haus** (*No. 7, www.stiftungbrandenburgertor.de, 030 22 63 30 30, closed Sat.–Sun.*), the former home of the German Impressionist painter, hosts rotating art exhibitions organized by the Brandenburg Gate Foundation. Established in 1696, the glass-fronted **Akademie der Künste** (Academy of Arts; see p. 36) hosts exhibitions across a number of disciplines, including photography, fine art, and architecture. To escape the crowds for a moment, head to the **Room of Silence** (*www.raum-der-stille-im-brandenburger-tor.de*) on the north side of the Brandenburg Gate, built specifically for visitors to rest and reflect on the city's troubled history.

Pariser Platz • S-Bahn/U-Bahn: Brandenburger Tor

UNTER DEN LINDEN & AROUND

Holocaust Monument

3 Some 2,700 concrete slabs occupy Peter Eisenman's enormous **Stelenfeld** (Field of Staele) at the **Denkmal für die ermordeten Juden Europas** (Monument for the Murdered Jews of Europe). The slabs—unmistakable in their association with sarcophagi—differ in height and sit in neat rows on an undulating floor. Walk directly off the street and among the staele, following the narrow paths as they dip and rise. An **Ort der Information** (Information Center; *closed Mon., Jan. 1, and Dec. 24–26*) beneath the monument pays personal tribute to the Jewish victims of the Holocaust. You'll see their names projected onto walls and can watch more than 150 video interviews with survivors (in English translation). Across the road on Ebertstrasse, the **Denkmal für die im Nationalsozialismus verfolgten Homosexuellen** (Memorial to Homosexuals Persecuted under Nazism) consists of a concrete cube showing alternating looped films of gay couples kissing.

Cora-Berliner-Strasse 1 • www.stiftung-denkmal.de • 030 26 39 43 • S-Bahn/U-Bahn: Brandenburger Tor

The Holocaust Monument is intended to provoke feelings of disorientation and unease.

A mini-world in itself, the vast, eco-friendly Sony Center on Potsdamer Platz contains an IMAX cinema, theaters, nightclubs, restaurants, offices, and apartments, and 130 shops.

Potsdamer Platz

Celebrated as one of Europe's most vibrant squares during the 1920s, what was left of Potsdamer Platz after the Allied bombings of World War II was leveled to make way for the Berlin Wall in 1961. After the fall of the wall, major investors including Daimler-Benz AG and Sony commissioned a team of internationally renowned architects led by Renzo Piano and Christoph Kohlbecker to catapult the square into the 21st century. What you see today is a dynamic commercial space that is distinguished by its soaring modernist skyscrapers. The glass-and-chrome offices of **Deutsche Bahn** (*No. 2*) and the **Art Deco Ritz-Carlton Hotel** (*No. 3*) are among the 19 buildings erected in what has become a thriving district in its own right. The square's "spiritual" centerpiece is the gleaming **Sony Center** (*www.sonycenter.de*), host venue for the world famous **Berlinale** film festival (see p. 102). Continuing the cinematic theme, the center's **Deutsche Kinemathek** (Film and Television Museum; see p. 29) presents an interactive look at the history of German cinema and TV. At the square's northeastern corner, the brown-brick **Kollhoff-Tower** *(No. 1)* boasts the fastest elevator in Europe (24 stories in 20 seconds), and it's a journey well worth making. A **Panoramapunkt** *(www.panoramapunkt.de, 030 25 93 70 80, €€, closed Dec. 24)* occupies the 24th and 25th stories of the building. Its 360-degree viewing platform promises views over the city as far as the eye can see. While here, you should also take a look at the venue's outdoor exhibition, which details the colorful history of the square.

Potsdamer Platz • www.potsdamerplatz.de • S-Bahn/U-Bahn: Potsdamer Platz

Checkpoint Charlie

5 Checkpoint Charlie was one of the most famous crossing points between East and West Berlin during the Cold War. Nowadays, the former checkpoint is still there—or at least an imitation of it—right down to the uniformed "guards" and a copy of the famous "YOU ARE NOW LEAVING THE AMERICAN SECTOR" sign. At the site, the **MauerMuseum: Museum Haus am Checkpoint Charlie** (Wall Museum: Museum House at Checkpoint Charlie; *www.mauermuseum.de, 30 25 37 25 0, €€€*) emphasizes the "human freedom" aspect of the wall years. The museum showcases the creative ways in which East Berliners tried to escape the GDR (DDR) regime. Highlights include extraordinary personal tales and exhibits of hot-air balloons, vehicles with concealed compartments, and a one-man submarine. More general exhibits hinge on the concepts of freedom and nonviolent protest and include pages from Mohandas Gandhi's diary.

SAVVY **TRAVELER**

If you were expecting to see the real Checkpoint Charlie, you needn't be disappointed. The original is currently housed in Dahlem's **AlliiertenMuseum** (see pp. 160–161), among other exhibits from the postwar Allied occupation.

Friedrichstrasse 43–45 • U-Bahn: Kochstrasse

KunstHalle

6 The program at this cutting-edge and challenging gallery draws on the extensive Corporate Art Collection of the Deutsche Bank, as well as cooperations with international partner museums, cultural institutions, and independent curators. As such, the KunstHalle features four key exhibitions a year focusing on the phenomenon of a globalized society and presents newly discovered works from artists working in "nontraditional" art centers like Asia, Africa, South America, and the Middle East. Shows to date have included Indonesian artists as well as "Artist of the Year" Imran Qureshi from Pakistan. Arrive in time to join a short, free tour of the intimate and minimal art space on Mondays *(available in English, 11 a.m.–8 p.m.)* or a tour-plus-lunch deal on Wednesdays *(1 p.m., €€€).*

Unter den Linden 13–15 • www.deutsche-bank-kunsthalle.de • 030 20 20 93 0 • €€ (free admission Mon.) • Closed Dec. 24–25 • U-Bahn: Französische Strasse

Curators make innovative use of space at the minimalist KunstHalle.

Bebelplatz

7 Bebelplatz is one of Unter den Linden's most handsome squares. At its heart, barely visible until you're almost on top of it, you'll find a memorial to the book burning of May 10, 1933. On that day the Nazis ritually set fire to more than 20,000 "degenerate" works, including books by Thomas Mann, Heinrich Heine, and Karl Marx. The memorial, by Micha Ullman, consists of a subterranean, glass-covered **Leere Bibliothek**—an empty library with enough shelving to hold all 20,000 books, it's said. Set into the ground close by, you'll see an associated plaque bearing an engraving of a line from Heinrich Heine, which translates as: "Where they burn books, they ultimately burn people." If you're visiting in summer, you may catch a free, open-air **Staatsoper für alle** concert, organized by the state opera company in June (*from 1 p.m., check website for details; www.staatsoper-berlin.de*). Crowds of more than 30,000 people gather to enjoy this "opera for all."

Bebelplatz • U-Bahn: Französische Strasse

GOOD **EATS**

■ **CHIPPS**
This smart-chic concept diner matches a stylish gray-walled interior with healthy, imaginative meals cooked in, and served from, an open kitchen.
Jägerstrasse 35, 030 28 08 80 6, €€

■ **ISHIN**
Boasting a spacious, unfussy interior, this is one of the best value-for-money restaurants in the area, and one of the only places to get really good sushi.
Mittelstrasse 24, 030 20 67 48 29, €

■ **LUTTER & WEGNER**
Overlooking Gendarmenmarkt, this restaurant serves refined German-Austrian food and has one of the best schnitzels in the city. There is a great wine list, which is also available if you dine at the adjacent bistro.
Charlottenstrasse 56, 030 20 29 54 0, €€€

Neue Wache

8 En route from Bebelplatz to the **Deutsches Historisches Museum** you'll pass the New Guardhouse. Karl Friedrich Schinkel's neoclassical guardhouse was originally built for the troops of the crown prince of Prussia. Step inside the building to see an enlarged version of Käthe Kollwitz's sculpture *Mother With Her Dead Son.* A shaft of light coming in through an oculus in the roof dramatically illuminates the sculpture on sunny days.

Unter den Linden 4 • U-Bahn: Französische Strasse

Deutsches Historisches Museum

9 The German Historical Museum is housed in Unter den Linden's oldest building, a 300-year-old baroque armory. Spanning 2,000 years of German history, the museum is organized chronologically and covers nine major eras from the Dark Ages to the present day. To avoid feeling overwhelmed by the sheer volume of the 8,000 items on show, it is best to focus on just one or two eras—the Reformation and the Thirty Years' War, the days of the German Empire, the Weimar Republic, or Divided Germany, for example. Audioguides, available in English at the ticket office (€3), offer greater insight into a selection of highlights per era and help to build a picture of life in Germany at the time.

Supplementing the permanent exhibition, an annex designed by architect I. M. Pei displays temporary shows throughout the year on subjects as diverse as the 1813 Battle of Leipzig or a retrospective of photojournalism in the former GDR (DDR).

Unter den Linden 2 • www.dhm.de • 030 20 30 44 44 • €€ • Closed Dec. 24 • U-Bahn: Französische Strasse

Gendarmenmarkt

10 Two near-identical, 18th-century churches face each other at opposite ends of this opulent and lively square. The **Französischer Dom,** erected to serve the city's French Huguenot community, now houses a museum dedicated to Huguenot history—the **Hugenottenmuseum** (030 22 91 76 0, €, closed Mon.). Come prepared to climb the 294 steps to the church's viewing platform (€) and you'll be rewarded with spectacular views over the city. If you've no head for heights, but an interest in politics, the **Deutscher Dom** (030 22 73 04 31, closed Mon.) houses five stories of German parliamentary history. Flanking

IN **THE KNOW**

Berlin's Mitte (center) can, depending on who you're talking to, refer to the trendy "downtown" section south of Torstrasse (known formerly as the Spandauer Vorstadt) or a broader area incorporating Alexanderplatz and Museumsinsel. The borough "Mitte" also includes Tiergarten and Wedding.

Schinkel's Konzerthaus (left) and the Französischer Dom (right) provide an elegant backdrop for the many visitors who come to the Gendarmenmarkt to socialize at the square's cafés.

the square between the two churches is the striking **Konzerthaus** *(www.konzerthaus.de, 030 20 30 92 10 1),* built by royal architect Karl Friedrich Schinkel in 1821. Home to the Konzerthausorchester Berlin, it's regarded as one of the finest music venues in the city. Four main halls—sumptuously decorated in period style—host more than 500 concerts a year, from symphonies and chamber music to musical theater and children's concerts. Check the website for events during your stay. In front of the entrance, stop to admire the **Schiller Monument** honoring the late 18th-century German *Sturm und Drang* (Storm and Stress) poet, Johann Christoph Friedrich von Schiller. Here, the poet stands above four allegorical figures sitting at his feet, each one representing an area of his work: history, lyric poetry, philosophy, and tragedy.

Gendarmenmarkt • U-Bahn: Hausvogteiplatz

Reichstag

*Germany's national parliamentary building is a jewel in
the crown of Berlin's 21st-century makeover.*

The dome's mirrored sculpture reflects light into the parliamentary chambers below.

Destroyed by fire, devastated by Allied bombing during World War II, and
ignored for decades by the Nazis and the former GDR (DDR; both of whom
based their parliaments elsewhere), Germany's Reichstag (parliament)
building has had it far from easy. British architect Sir Norman Foster added
the iconic glass dome during his post-reunification refurbishment of the
building. The dome, now a fixture on the Berlin skyline, has come to symbolize
the progressive transparency of a reunited Germany.

UNTER DEN LINDEN & AROUND

■ OLD MEETS NEW

The Reichstag forms part of the **Regierungsviertel,** or Government Quarter—a string of buildings whose clean, modern lines and extensive use of glass reflect the openness and transparency of the modern government. On arrival, scrutinize the Reichstag's imposing neobaroque exterior to see the 1916 inscription *Dem Deutschen Volke* (To the German People), as well as a number of bullet holes deliberately preserved as part of the old-meets-new restoration strategy.

On entering the building, see how its interior balances architectural glass-and-steel gestures with imposing Greek columns and preserved "victory graffiti" scribbled onto the walls by Soviet soldiers following the Battle of Berlin in 1945. Take the elevator to the roof terrace at the base of the dome.

■ BREAKFAST AT THE DOME

The Reichstag is the only parliament building in the world with a public dining area, but you need to book in advance to eat at the Käfer rooftop restaurant *(030 22 62 99 33, €€€)*. Try the breakfast, then sit back and enjoy the views from the terrace.

SAVVY **TRAVELER**

Visitors to the dome must register in advance. All tours are free and can be arranged at the nearby Service Center (beside the Berlin Pavilion on the south side of Scheidemannstrasse), but waiting times can be long. It is best to book online ahead of your trip.

■ A TOUR OF THE DOME

Inside the dome, a mirrored, cone-shaped light sculpture dominates the space. Around its base, you can read a short account of the building's history. Then peer down into the parliamentary debating chambers; the dome sits directly above them. Pick up a free audioguide when you are ready to climb the 755-foot-long (230 m) staircase that winds elegantly around the interior of the glass dome. Lasting 20 minutes and triggered by proximity sensors, the audioguide describes the dramatic and fascinating history of the building, including the time artists wrapped it entirely in polypropylene (1995). The guide also draws attention to a number of visible landmarks outside the building. Once at the top, you can enjoy the 360-degree panorama of the city.

UNTER DEN LINDEN & AROUND

Platz der Republik 1 • www.bundestag.de • 030 30 22 73 21 52 • Closed Dec. 24 • S-Bahn/U-Bahn: Brandenburger Tor

The Golden Twenties

The Berlin of the 1920s was modern and exciting. Home to many artists and writers, it was famous for its wild nightlife—the bars and cabarets immortalized in the film *The Blue Angel* and the musical *Cabaret*. Given the terrible loss of life in the preceding World War I and the horrors of World War II to follow, it is no surprise that this decade is fondly remembered as "The Golden Twenties."

M. Friedlaender's Berlin café scene captures the louche atmosphere of the city during the 1920s.
Opposite: Marlene Dietrich as Lola Lola in *Der blaue Engel* (*The Blue Angel*).

By November 1918, World War I was over, the Kaiser had abdicated, and revolution was in the air. A republic had been declared and a battle for power was underway. Elections held early in 1919 gave victory to the Social Democrats led by Friedrich Ebert. The government fled the maelstrom of Berlin politics for the relative safety of Weimar, 120 miles (193 km) to the southeast. The new Weimar Constitution, adopted in August 1919, was full of hope, optimism, and equality. But it was overly idealistic, for these were times of mass unemployment, widespread poverty, and rampant hyperinflation. The days were marked by riots, strikes, and street combat between the Nazis and the communists. This turbulence persisted: During the next 14 years there would be 17 changes of government and 13 chancellors.

Berlin entered a phase of liberalism in society and the arts, attracting young, fresh, and daring supporters. Unfettered by censorship, they were eager to explore and exploit Berlin's newfound freedoms. Among them was the dancer Anita Berber. A rising star of an avant-garde cabaret scene, Anita kept a suite of rooms at the Hotel Adlon on Pariser Platz. After her evening performances she'd head for the five-star hotels on Unter den Linden, wearing an ankle-length sable coat that she dared the maître d's to take to the cloakroom—she wore nothing underneath.

Come to the Cabaret

Cabaret thrived in many forms, performers, composers, and lyricists becoming household names. They included openly lesbian singer Claire Waldoff, with her gruff persona and repertoire of 300 songs, as well as Margo Lion and a young Marlene Dietrich. Their flirtatious duet "Wenn die beste Freundin" ("When my Best Girlfriend") was a smash hit of the day. Club-goers could see Trude Hesterberg, Kate

MARLENE **DIETRICH**

Born in the Schöneberg district of Berlin, Dietrich started her career in the chorus line, making her first stage appearance in 1922. She shot to international stardom following her leading role in *Der blaue Engel (The Blue Angel)*, the first major German talkie. At the time, producers and directors from Hollywood were flocking to Berlin's UFA studios, where cutting-edge techniques were being perfected. One producer, Josef von Sternberg, persuaded Dietrich to move to Hollywood with him, where she became an icon of the silver screen.

Christopher Isherwood (above left) moved to Berlin in the late 1920s. He was lured by descriptions of life in the city in letters he received from his school friend, the poet W. H. Auden (above right), who had been living in Berlin for eight months.
Opposite: Cover of *Lustige Blätter* magazine

Kühl, or the outrageous Wilhelm Bendow. By 1925, Conrad Veidt, who had spent the first few years of the decade working the Ku'damm dressed as a girl, was Germany's highest paid film actor.

Berlin's nightlife attracted artists, writers, and performers from all over Europe, among them Erich Kästner, Klaus and Erika Mann, Jean Cocteau, André Gide, and Ernest Hemingway. Josephine Baker arrived from Paris in 1925, bringing "La Revue Negre" to the Theater des Westens. She became an overnight sensation. It was said that after seeing Baker, the women of Berlin were never the same again.

A City of Women

For it *was* a city of women: World War I had wiped out a generation of men and boys. Women were wanted and needed in the workforce, giving them personal and financial freedoms they'd never experienced before. Working women had their own apartments, bank accounts, social lives, and wardrobes purchased at the newly affordable department stores springing up all over the city.

Writers and Artists

Bertolt Brecht lived in Schöneberg, where he wrote the lyrics for composer Kurt Weill's *Die Dreigroschenoper (The Threepenny Opera)*. A young British writer, Christopher Isherwood, arrived in March 1929. It was while living on Nollendorfstrasse that he recorded the events of everyday life in his diaries. Reworked as fiction, they'd become his two Berlin novels, *Mr Norris Changes Trains* and *Goodbye To Berlin*. The latter forms the basis of the stage and screen musical *Cabaret*, which introduced the world to Sally Bowles, a singer lost in the heady world of Weimar Berlin, portrayed on screen in 1973 by Liza Minnelli.

Dawn of Darkness

In Berlin, the only constant was change. A succession of failed governments gave rise to the far right. Banks collapsed and unemployment rose. Five general elections were held in 1932 against a backdrop of social reform that included a campaign to curtail what Berlin was most famous for—its wild nightlife. Clubs, bars, and cabarets were raided and those allowed to remain open had their opening hours reduced. At the end of January 1933, the elderly German President Paul von Hindenburg appointed Adolf Hitler as chancellor. The National Socialists were in power, and the Weimar Republic was finished.

THE REAL **WEIMAR**

For artists like George Grosz and Otto Dix the harsh realities of postwar Weimar society were all too real. In many of their works, Berlin life is depicted as sordid and seedy. Grosz's fat-cat businessmen and half-naked women wander dangerous streets, while Dix's *Portrait of the Dancer, Anita Berber,* painted in 1925, is now one of the most iconic images of the era. Here, the dancer poses with attitude and lips as red as the dress she wears.

Brunch

Many Berliners like to stay out into the wee hours and sleep late, so it's no surprise that brunch has a special place in their hearts. Virtually every neighborhood has a decent selection of brunch spots, ranging from traditional German platters to generous Russian, Italian, and Mediterranean buffets.

■ CAFÉ IM DEUTSCHEN HISTORISCHEN MUSEUM

Located separately from the main building at the German Historical Museum on Unter den Linden, this pleasant café has a spacious interior and a wonderful outdoor terrace that looks across the Spree River to the Berliner Dom. The menu focuses on regional dishes and local produce, with brunch options such as the "Zeughaus" (cheese and cold meats, smoked salmon, and boiled egg).

Unter den Linden 2 • www.koflerkompanie.com • 030 20 64 27 44 • € • U-Bahn: Französische Strasse

■ BARCOMI'S

This buzzy café and delicatessen in the Scheunenviertel district is a perennial favorite with Mitte locals. Owned by American cookbook author, Cynthia Barcomi, this place serves up breakfasts and bagels with an American twist, as well as a heavenly cheesecake and a great selection of house-roasted coffees.

Sophie-Gips-Höfe, Sophienstrasse 21 • www.barcomis.de • 030 28 59 83 63 • € • U-Bahn: Weinmeisterstrasse

■ CAFÉ AM LITERATURHAUS

Occupying a delightful turn-of-the-20th-century villa on an elegant side street off the bustling Ku'damm in Charlottenburg, this café-restaurant has a refined breakfast and lunch menu that extends from amaranth muesli and pancakes to smoked salmon on rye with poached eggs.

Fasanenstrasse 23 • 030 88 25 41 • € • U-Bahn: Uhlandstrasse

■ PASTERNAK

Located on the corner of a leafy square in Berlin's east, the quaintly atmospheric Pasternak serves the best

Brunch at Café Bastard in Kreuzberg

Russian-themed Sunday brunch in the city. From 9 a.m. the serving tables are filled with mountains of blinis, quail's eggs, caviar, and salmon—not to mention several exquisite desserts.

Knaackstrasse 22/24 • www.restaurant-pasternak.de • 030 44 13 39 • € • U-Bahn: Senefelderplatz

■ CAFÉ BASTARD

An artfully arranged platter of cold meats, cheeses, and seasonal fruits is the popular choice at Kreuzberg's Café Bastard. Each comes with a basket of bread—freshly baked in an in-house stone oven. Optional extras include a boiled egg or some homemade jam.

Reichenberger Strasse 122 • 030 54 82 18 66 • € • U-Bahn: Kottbusser Tor

■ CAFÉ MORGENLAND

The weekend brunch in this Kreuzberg café is something of an institution. The Mediterranean-themed spread includes Middle Eastern and Turkish treats of salads and stuffed vegetables as well as meatballs, eggs, freshly baked breads, homemade dips, and pancakes.

Skalitzer Strasse 35 • www.morgenland-berlin.de • 030 61 13 29 1 • € • U-Bahn: Görlitzer Bahnhof

Around Museumsinsel

Nestled between the Spree River to the east and the Spreekanal (canal) to the west, Museumsinsel (Museum Island) combines 19th-century neoclassical architecture with a calm riverside ambiance and five outstanding museums. Between them, the museums house more than 2,000 years of cultural history from around the world, and include such treasures as the Pergamon Altar from ancient Greece and a world-famous bust of the ancient Egyptian, Nefertiti. Within striking distance, Alexanderplatz holds an altogether different fascination. Its vast, windswept landscape flanked by high-rise blocks and punctuated by the space-age Fernsehturm (TV Tower) epitomizes Soviet bravado of the 1960s. Between Museumsinsel and Alexanderplatz lies the Nikolaiviertel, Berlin's historic center—a cluster of streets with a number of small, but charming, sights.

◐ **The Bode-Museum sits
at the northern end of
Museumsinsel, where
the Spree River and
Spreekanal converge.**

Around Museumsinsel

*Dazzling skyline views and the pick of Berlin's
top museums are the highlights of this compact tour.*

❶ Pergamonmuseum (see pp. 74–75) Tour the
galleries of this museum dedicated to the ancient
worlds of the Middle East and marvel at their
treasures from antiquity. Head next door.

❷ Neues Museum (see
pp. 82–85) Admire the
architecture as well as the
exhibits at the New Museum.
Take a break in the pretty
Pleasure Garden before
continuing on Am Lustgarten.

❸ Berliner Dom (see pp. 76) Climb the magnificent
dome for views across central Berlin. Continue east,
passing through Marx-Engels-Forum.

❹ Alexanderplatz (see p. 77) Take in the Soviet-style
features of this historic square and former GDR (DDR)
landmark before exiting the square on the southern side.

**AROUND MUSEUMSINSEL DISTANCE: 2.5 MILES (4 KM)
TIME: APPROX. 8 HOURS S-BAHN START: HACKESCHER MARKT**

9 Hackesche Höfe (see pp. 80–81) Unwind at this network of refurbished art nouveau courtyards housing galleries, restaurants, theaters, and more.

8 Haus Schwarzenberg (see p. 80) Soak up the postwar atmosphere of this scruffy, unrefurbished courtyard and reflect on its small but powerful contents. You'll find the Hackesche Höfe next door.

7 Zille Museum (see p. 79) Chuckle over the satirical cartoons of much-loved illustrator Heinrich Zille. Return to Alexanderplatz and head north on Spandauer Strasse to Rosenthaler Strasse.

6 Knoblauchhaus (see pp. 78–79) Get a feel for life in Biedermeier Berlin. Continue on Poststrasse and head south on Propstrasse.

Rosenthaler Platz

LINIENSTRASSE
ROSENTHALER STR.
GORMANNSTR.
ROSA-LUXEMBURG-STR.
Rosa-Luxemburg-Platz
TORSTRASSE
MOLLSTRASSE
KARL-LIEBKNECHT STR.
WADZECKSTR.
OTTO-BRAUN-STRASSE

Weinmeisterstr.

9 Hackesche Höfe
8 Haus Schwarzenberg

MÜNZSTRASSE
DIRCKSENSTRASSE
ROCHSTR.

Hackescher Markt

Alexanderplatz
Alexanderplatz
4 ALEXANDER-PLATZ
Alexanderplatz

Fernsehturm

Berliner Dom
3
MARX-ENGELS-FORUM
SCHLOSSPLATZ

SPANDAUER STR.
Rotes Rathaus
GRUNERSTR.
ALEXANDERSTRASSE

Zille Museum **7** **5**
NIKOLAIVIERTEL
Klosterstr.
6 **Nikolaikirche**
Knoblauchhaus

Jannowitzbr.
Jannowitzbr.

Spree
Spreekanal
GERTRAUDENSTR.
FISCHERINSEL
MÄRKISCHES UFER
RUNGESTR.
BRÜCKENSTRASSE
WALLSTRASSE
Märkisches Museum
Spittelmarkt
SEYDELSTRASSE
ALTE JAKOBSTR.
ANNENSTR.
Heinrich-Heine-Strasse
KÖPENICKER STR.

5 Nikolaikirche (see p. 78) Sample the delights of the Nikolaiviertel, starting with its eponymous church. Walk to the southern end of Nikolaikirchplatz.

Pergamonmuseum

1 With three distinct and rich collections across as many interconnected floors, the Pergamon Museum is the most visited museum in the whole city. Consider buying tickets online in advance of your trip (see sidebar opposite). There is a great deal to see here, although sadly the main attraction, the **Pergamonaltar** (Pergamon Altar) is out of action until 2019 owing to the reconstruction works that will make the Pergamonmuseum a focal point for the whole Museum Island.

Disappointment will be short-lived, however, if you head straight for the Roman Art galleries and the **Market Gate of Miletus,** a 98.5-foot-wide (30 m) marble monument from the second century A.D., with ornate friezes featuring bull and flower reliefs. The 46-by-98.5-foot (14 by 30 m) **Ishtar Gate**—the eighth gate to the inner city of Babylon (575 B.C.), once considered one

A reconstruction of the Ishtar Gate, one of several gates to the ancient city of Babylon

of the Seven Wonders of the World—and associated Processional Way from Babylon is another highlight.

Besides these monumental exhibits, an impressively vast main hall hosts the **Antikensammlung** (Collection of Classical Antiquities), some of which is also held in the Neues Museum (see p. 84) and whose origins hark back to the 17th century. Among the exhibits here are sculptures, mosaics, pottery, and architecture from the archaic to Hellenistic ages.

On the first floor, the **Museum für Islamische Kunst** (Islamic Art Museum) shows artwork from the 8th to the 19th centuries, including the **Mshatta Facade,** which originates from the unfinished Qasr Mshatta or Mshatta palace located south of Amman in present-day Jordan. Also here is part of the expansive **Keir Collection,** which includes exquisite carpets, textiles, manuscripts, ceramics, and more. Head down to the museum's basement for the **Vorderasiatisches Museum** (Middle East Museum), for objects found within areas of Assyrian, Sumerian, and Babylonian culture.

Bodestrasse 1 • www.smb.museum • 030 26 64 24 24 2 • €€€ • Closed Dec. 24 • S-Bahn: Hackescher Markt

Neues Museum

2 See pp. 82–85.

Bodestrasse 1–3 • www.smb.museum • 030 20 90 51 01 • €€€ • Closed Dec. 24 • S-Bahn: Hackescher Markt

SAVVY **TRAVELER**

Entry to Museum Island is free with the **Berlin WelcomeCard and Museum Island pass** (see p. 175). You can also buy tickets for individual museums or a **Bereichskarte Museumsinsel** *(a combo-ticket for the day; €€€€).* Buy online to book yourself into a specific time slot. Note that the island is undergoing reconstruction and check the shared website *(www.smb .museum)* for developments.

Besides the **Pergamonmuseum** and the **Neues Museum,** the island boasts:

The **Alte Nationalgalerie** (Old National Gallery; *Bodestrasse 1–3, 030 26 64 24 40 1, €€€, closed Mon., Dec. 24 and Dec. 31),* with one of Germany's most significant collections of 19th-century art;

The **Altes Museum** (Old Museum; *Am Lustgarten, 030 26 64 24 24 2, €€€, closed Mon., Dec. 24 and 31),* with a wonderful rotunda as well as ancient artifacts from the Greek, Roman, and Etruscan eras;

The **Bode-Museum** *(Am Kupfergraben 1, 030 26 64 24 24 2, €€€, closed Mon., Dec. 24 and 31),* with a collection of art and artifacts from the Byzantine and medieval periods.

AROUND MUSEUMSINSEL

Berliner Dom

3 Modeled on St. Peter's in Vatican City, the exterior of the Protestant Berlin Cathedral, all ornate facades, granite stairs, and grandiose carved doors, is a blend of baroque and Italian Renaissance styles. No less dramatic on the inside, the cathedral's 230-foot-high (70 m) dome draws all eyes upward. Follow the "*Zur Kuppel*" signs to climb its 270 steps and you'll be rewarded with close-ups of the intricate 500,000-piece mosaics portraying the beatitudes from the Sermon on the Mount. At the top, the views across Berlin are breathtaking.

The nave is richly decorated, too. Of special note are pillars featuring the four main Protestant reformers (Luther, Melanchthon, Zwingli, and Calvin), reliefs illustrating events from the lives of the apostles, and a richly decorated chancel with an altar designed by Prussian architect Friedrich August Stüler. Admire the chancel's stained glass and oak pulpit. The **Sauer organ** (named after its builder) is the largest late-Romantic organ in the world in its original condition and is a pleasure to hear—check the website for recital times, or purchase a recording in the cathedral.

The **Baptismal and Matrimonial Chapel** adjacent to the main hall contains a small museum with designs and models that document the planning and building of the cathedral. In the crypt you'll find sarcophagi spanning 500 years, including those of 18th-century Prussian emperor Frederick I and his queen, Sophia. Outside, take a moment to enjoy the **Lustgarten** (Pleasure Garden), once a vegetable garden for the nearby Berliner Schloss (Royal Palace; see p. 119).

Am Lustgarten • www.berlinerdom.de • 030 20 26 91 36 • €€ (audioguide €3) • S-Bahn: Hackescher Markt

GOOD **EATS**

■ **CAFÉ OLIV**
This modern, airy café has a focus on organic and regional ingredients, and serves homemade sandwiches, soups, and delicious baked goods. **Münzstrasse 8, 030 89 20 65 40, €**

■ **ZUR LETZTEN INSTANZ**
Established in 1621, this is Berlin's oldest—and perhaps coziest—restaurant and once served Napoleon. The menu boasts traditional specialties such as grilled pork knuckle and Buletten (meat patties). **Waisenstrasse 14–16, 030 24 25 52 8, €€**

■ **ZUM NUSSBAUM**
A copy of one of the city's oldest pubs, this is a series of small, wood-paneled rooms. The menu features hearty German fare such as schnitzels, bockwurst, and potato salad. **Am Nussbaum 3, 030 24 23 09 5, €€**

Alexanderplatz

4 Just over a half a mile (1 km) east of Museumsinsel, yet a world away in terms of feel and architectural aesthetic, Alexanderplatz is one of Berlin's most historic squares and an important relic from the GDR (DDR) era. Often referred to simply as "Alex" by locals, the square is surrounded by the concrete *Plattenbauten* (modular high-rises) so typical of Soviet urban planning. Today, everything from newspaper offices to nightclubs occupy the buildings. A number of the square's communist-era structures have become protected landmarks, starting with the towering **Park Inn Hotel** (*No. 7*) and the **Galeria Kaufhof** department store (*No. 9*), both in the northwestern corner.

Walk east across the square to find two more—the **Weltzeituhr** (World Clock) and the **Brunnen der Völkerfreundschaft** (Fountain of International Friendship), both popular meeting points. South of here is the square's literal highlight, the 1,200-foot-tall (365 m) **Fernsehturm** (TV Tower; *Panoramastrasse 1a, www.tv-turm.de, 030 24 75 75 87 5, €€€*), which features a rotating café-restaurant and a viewing platform with some of the best vistas in the city. To take a break from the square's Soviet-style architecture, step into the 13th-century **Marienkirche** (Church of St Mary; *Karl-Liebknecht-Strasse, www.marienkirche-berlin.de, 030 24 75 95 10*), beside the Fernsehturm, which boasts the 72-foot-long (22 m) **"Totentanz"** (Dance of Death) fresco that dates back to the 15th century.

The Weltzeituhr in Alexanderplatz displays the time in major cities around the world.

Between Karl-Liebknecht-Strasse and Rathausstrasse • U-Bahn: Alexanderplatz

IN **THE KNOW**

The **Nikolaiviertel,** Berlin's historic center, underwent an intriguing architectural makeover during the former GDR (DDR) years. Rebuilt in 1987 to commemorate the city's 750th anniversary, the district aims to capture the aura of the Middle Ages and yet is built using the modular structures typical of East German architecture at the time.

Nikolaikirche

5 The late-Gothic St. Nicholas's Church stands at the heart of the **Nikolaiviertel,** a reconstruction of Berlin's medieval center. The oldest church in Berlin, it was originally built between 1220 and 1230, but suffered severe damage during World War II. No longer used for services, today the church functions mainly as a museum and, occasionally, a concert venue. As you walk around it today—inside and out—it is impossible not to admire its faithful restoration during the 1980s. To discover more on the history of the church, head for the broad Gothic nave and 15th-century ambulatory, home to a permanent exhibition entitled **"Vom Stadtgrund bis zur Doppelspitze"** ("From the Foundation of the City to the Twin Spires"), complete with an interactive display. Parts of the church that did survive the war include a 14th-century bronze baptismal font and a handsome 18th-century pulpit. In the crypt you'll find a collection of medieval coins, graphic artworks, and medallions—lost during the war and recovered in the 1990s.

Nikolaikirchplatz 1 • www.stadtmuseum.de/nikolaikirche • 030 24 00 21 62 • €€ (audioguide €2) • U-Bahn: Altes Stadthaus

Knoblauchhaus

6 Journey back in time to the Biedermeier era of the early 19th century with a tour of this former family home. The Knoblauchs were members of the new urban elite that came to define this period. Almost all of this three-story baroque town house erected in 1760 is original, making it one of very few such buildings still standing in Berlin today. It also housed the Knoblauch family business, which was connected to the silk industry. All of the rooms here feature original furnishings from the era—paintings, silverware, chandeliers . . . even a piano and an old bicycle—as well as pictures and documents that reveal elements of the Knoblauchs' privileged social lives in Berlin. While it is possible to visit the museum on your own, book in advance to join an hour-long tour given (*free*) in English to appreciate the full impact of the Biedermeier era on German society.

Poststrasse 23 • www.stadtmuseum.de/knoblauchhaus • 030 24 00 21 62 • Closed Mon. • U-Bahn: Altes Stadthaus

Zille Museum

7 This small venue is dedicated to Heinrich Zille, a much-loved chronicler of Berlin's backstreets during the Weimar years—you'll pass a statue of the bearded artist as you approach. Once described by journalist Kurt Tucholsky as the "purest incarnation of Berlin," Zille's work often depicted the city's poorer inhabitants going about their daily lives. A permanent exhibition features many original works, including his famous **Children of the Street** cartoons as well as paintings of prostitutes who used to work in nearby streets a century ago. Pop to the store for imaginative Zille-themed trinkets, postcards, and associated literature. Afterward, head to Zille's (authentically re-created) favorite *Kneipe* (bar), the nearby **Zum Nussbaum** (see sidebar p. 76).

Propstrasse 11 • 030 24 63 25 00 • €€ • U-Bahn: Altes Stadthaus

Heinrich Zille's skill lay in capturing the characteristics of Berlin's social stereotypes.

Haus Schwarzenberg

8 Schwarzenberg House is an unrefurbished courtyard with a compelling postwar aura and surrounded by small but significant museums that explore Jewish life in the area during the Third Reich. **Gedenkstätte Stille Helden** (*030 23 45 79 19*) commemorates German heroes (*Helden*) who risked their lives to save persecuted Jews, and documents the successes as well as the tragic failures through photographs, reports, and oral testimonies. Among these heroes was Otto Weidt, a German entrepreneur whose brush-making workshop—which employed blind Jewish workers—is located next door and is now the **Museum Blindenwerkstatt Otto Weidt** (*www.museum-blindenwerkstatt.de, 030 28 59 94 07*). Weidt helped hide a number of his employees via a hidden room located behind a backless wardrobe. You can still see this room today, along with the rest of the workshop, which has been kept in its original condition. Farther toward the back of the courtyard is the **Anne Frank Zentrum** (*www.annefrank.de, 030 28 88 65 60 0, €€, closed Mon.*), which offers a modern, interactive exhibition exploring the life and experiences of Anne Frank, the Dutch teenage diarist whose family attempted to escape the Nazis by hiding in cramped rooms behind a concealed doorway at her father's warehouse in Amsterdam.

Rosenthaler Strasse 39 • S-Bahn: Hackescher Markt

Hackesche Höfe

9 Originally built in the 1900s and restored to its former art nouveau glory in 1997, the distinguished Hackesche Höfe offers a stark contrast to **Haus Schwarzenberg** (see above). This network of eight beautifully tiled and often ivy-clad courtyards (*Höfe*) is packed with places to shop, drink, eat, and people watch. Deserving special mention, **Endellscher Hof** is the first courtyard as you enter from Rosenthaler Strasse. Designed by art nouveau artist and architect August Endell, it features the **Chamäleon**

Theater *(www.chamaeleonberlin.com, 030 40 00 59 0)*, housed in an original tavern and offering everything from tap dancers to trapeze artists, and the **Hackescher Hof Restaurant** *(www.hackescher-hof .de, 030 28 35 29 3)*, which has a beautiful original ceiling.

The other courtyards are home to fashion boutiques, gift shops, and handicraft stores. Most of them stay open late (up to 9 p.m.), which adds to the unique, up-tempo evening vibe of the area. Browse some local favorites: **Artificium** *(Hof 2, 030 30 87 22 80)*, specializing in 20th-century photography, dance, design, and architecture; **Trippen** *(Hof 6, www.trippen.com, 030 28 39 13 37)*—the last word in avant-garde shoes and bags; and **Coy Art to Wear** *(Hof 5, 030 65 79 84 96)*, with original hats designed by milliner Cornelia Plotzki. Round off your day with cocktails at hip bar, **Oxymoron** *(Hof 1, 030 28 39 18 86)*.

Rosenthaler Strasse 40–1 • S-Bahn: Hackescher Markt

Diners enjoy the laid-back atmosphere of the Endellscher Hof as passersby come and go.

Neues Museum

Ancient Egypt and early European history are the focus of this stunningly renovated venue on Museumsinsel.

Among the museum's most prized possessions is this ancient bust of Nefertiti.

Berlin's Neues Museum is both an architectural and a cultural attraction. Built in the 1850s, it suffered severe damage during World War II. Now fully renovated, today's incarnation incorporates many remnants from the original building, intricately melding the old with the new. The rooms, in part inspired by ancient Egyptian, Greek, Roman, and Byzantine designs, vary hugely, from square to circular, domed to vaulted, and are now peppered with a dizzying array of cultural treasures and historical curiosities.

MAIN HALL

You enter the museum via the vast, showstopping **Vestibule,** a medley of old, exposed brickwork, new installations of concrete and marble, and a timber roof. Pick up an audioguide—included in the admission price—from the cloakroom to the rear of the hall. The main wings of the building lead off from either side of this hall and surround two interior courtyards—the Greek and the Egyptian. Immediately opposite the entrance a grand staircase leads down to Level 0 with access to the Greek Courtyard, and up to Levels 2 and 3.

GREEK COURTYARD

Extending to the full height of the museum, this courtyard lies at the center of the museum's southern wing. Look up to see enormous busts of the ancient Greek god Zeus and goddesses Hera and Athena peering back down

IN **THE KNOW**

The work of David Chipperfield Architects, the refurbishment of the Neues Museum won the prestigious Mies van der Rohe Award in 2011. Take a virtual tour of the museum (*www.neues -museum.de*) to see the renovated rooms before they were filled with exhibits.

at you. The main feature here is the 19th-century **Schievelbein Frieze,** which graces all four walls of the courtyard, and in which you can follow the violent eruption of Mount Vesuvius in A.D. 79 and the subsequent destruction of the city of Pompeii.

EGYPTIAN MUSEUM AND PAPYRUS COLLECTION

Housed in the museum's northern wing and starting on Level 1, this collection holds some 2,500 artifacts, prefaced by a thorough historical overview of the collection and the discipline of Egyptology itself (Room 111). As you walk from one room to the next, note the boldly painted walls and ceilings—all remnants of the original interior.

Highlights of the collection include the **Berlin Green Head** (Room 109)—a 400 B.C. head of a priest carved from smooth green stone. The climax of the collection, however, is the 3,330-year-old **bust of Nefertiti,** the wife of the legendary pharoah Akhenaten, who reigned ca 1353–1336 B.C. Although the bust is displayed in a room of its own on Level 2 (Room 210), be prepared to jostle for a decent view of it. It is worth doing so, though, particularly as photography of the piece is strictly prohibited.

■ EGYPTIAN COURTYARD

At the center of the northern wing, this courtyard is similar in size to the Greek Courtyard, and access can be gained on all three levels. Of particular note is Level 1, which seeks to re-create the atmosphere of an Egyptian temple. Here are the remains of four murals from the original museum— ten others were destroyed during the war—depicting scenes from Karnak, Edfu, the island of Philae, and Abu Simbel. Head down to Level 0 to see 13 stone sarcophagi or up to Level 2 for treasures from the reign of Akhenaten.

■ MUSEUM OF PRE- AND EARLY HISTORY

With 6,000 objects on view, this collection occupies the southern wing of the museum. It offers a sweeping survey of archaeological finds from across Europe and parts of Asia from the Stone Age up to the Middle Ages, as well as objects from the **Antikensammlung** (an important collection of Greek and Roman antiquities; see also p. 75). On Level 1, there is an entire cabinet full of what looks like

rubble (Room 102). As you get closer, you'll see the twisted, fractured, and in part molten remains of artifacts that were among the thousands of treasures destroyed in Allied bombing raids in 1945.

Additional highlights of this collection include Heinrich Schliemann's collection of **artifacts from Troy** (Rooms 103–104) and a cultural history of neighboring **Cyprus** (Room 106).

Highlights on Level 2 include an ancient Roman bronze statue of the **Xanten Youth** (Room 201) and an immense statue of the **ancient Greek Sun god Helios** from the second century A.D. (Room 203). This last is the only exhibit occupying the beautiful, three-story, brick-walled **Southern Dome Room.**

■ LEVEL 3

Up on the newly reopened third floor, you'll find an exhibition called **Steinzeit, Bronzezeit, Eisenzeit** (Stone Age, Bronze Age, Iron Age), dedicated to the museum's prehistoric collection. Among the

A vase depicting the Egyptian god Bes, ca 1550–1070 B.C.

Looking down at the stone sarcophagi in Level 0 of the Egyptian Courtyard

highlights of the Stone Age is an elk found at Berlin's Hansaplatz in 1956 (Room 308), whose existence testifies to the dramatic climate change that occurred during that period. From the Bronze Age you will find the world-renowned **Berlin Golden Hat** (Room 305)—a conical item made of thin gold leaf that represents one of four similar items known from Bronze Age Europe. Displays from Iron Age cultures

have their own highlights, including Hallstatt-period graves (Room 302). If you have time for one exhibit only, head straight for the **"Time Machine"** river landscape (Room 304), where animated film sequences illustrate the lives of inhabitants from the landscape during the course of the preceding millennia. Created especially for the exhibition, the film includes many objects that feature in the museum's displays.

Bodestrasse 1–3 • www.smb.museum • 030 20 90 51 01 • €€€ • Closed Dec. 24 • S-Bahn: Hackescher Markt

Jewish Heritage

In 1945, barely a trace of the capital's Jewish heritage had survived. What the Nazis hadn't destroyed had been obliterated by Allied bombing. And yet Jewish Berlin survives today with the golden dome of the city's restored Neue Synagoge, in Oranienburger Strasse, one of the dominant sights of Berlin's skyline. Berlin also has one of the world's fastest-growing Jewish communities.

AROUND MUSEUMSINSEL

The placard pictured was erected at the Jewish Tietz store, Berlin, during the 1933 Nazi boycott of all things Jewish. It reads "Germans, defend yourselves, do not buy from Jews."
Opposite: The Neue Synagoge on Oranienburger Strasse

A Troubled History

Jews first settled in Berlin in the 13th century, and endured centuries-long cycles of repression. From the end of the 17th century, increasing toleration saw a steady increase to the city's Jewish population. By the 19th century, Berlin had become a center for liberal Jewish thinking, and at the turn of 20th century, there were more than 100,000 Jews in Berlin. The Weimar Era that followed World War I saw a cultural renaissance in the capital. Jewish politicians, writers, artists, and musicians were at the forefront of this cultural life. By this time, German Jews were largely middle class and well integrated in society. However, Berlin was also home to significant numbers of Eastern European Jews who had fled their shtetls because of pogroms. In start contrast, these Jews were poor, ghettoized, and spoke Yiddish.

Descent into Barbarity

When the Nazis came to power in 1933, Berlin had around 160,000 Jews. By 1939, 75,000 of them had been driven abroad. Another 8,000 managed to survive the Holocaust, hidden by their fellow citizens in attics and basements. For many, however, there followed the well-documented passage to the death camps through detention centers such as the Jewish Old People's Home on Grosse Hamburger Strasse and the railroad station at Grunewald.

Jewish Berlin Today

After 1945, few of those German Jews who did survive the Holocaust chose to remain in Berlin, and it was not until the end of the Cold War that the city's Jewish population began to rise again, partly owing to influxes from Eastern Europe and the former Soviet Union. Testimony to Berlin's thriving Jewish community today are its synagogues and Jewish schools, cultural centers, and restaurants.

STOLPER**STEINER**

Memorials can be found throughout Berlin and include **Places of Remembrance** in Schöneberg (see pp. 142–143). Perhaps most touching, however, are artist Gunter Demnig's *Stolpersteine* (Stumbling Blocks). Found throughout Nazi-occupied Europe, these small brass squares are set into sidewalks, each one a memorial to a Jewish inhabitant who perished during the Holocaust. Three such memorials lie at the entrance to the **Hackesche Höfe** *(Rosenthaler Strasse 40–41)*, in memory of Anita Bukofzer and Ury and Paula Davidson who died at Auschwitz.

The Riverside

Berlin's two primary rivers—the Spree and the Havel—are supplemented by a multitude of smaller canals and lakes to create a network of inner-city waterways that crisscross the city. Along the banks you'll find pleasant boat rides, waterfront dining, and a host of other outdoor activities.

AROUND MUSEUMSINSEL

■ BEST RIVER CRUISE
One of the most enjoyable ways to see the main sights of Berlin is by river. Berliner Wassersportund Service GmbH & Co. (BWSG) offer a one-hour cruise aboard an open-topped boat. The tour starts and ends at the Alte Börse pier, in the Museumsinsel neighborhood; book early morning or late afternoon to avoid the midday sun.

The tour heads east first, offering a dramatic close-up of the nearby **Berliner Dom** (see p. 76) and tantalizing glimpses of the medieval **Nikolaiviertel** (see p. 78). Turning at the Mühlendamm lock, the boat returns past the striking neoclassical facade of the **Altes Nationalgalerie** (see p. 75) and the distinctive dome of the **Bode-Museum** (see p. 75), before passing by Friedrichstrasse and the former Berlin Wall checkpoint. Cruising past the **Reichstag** (see pp. 62–63), the tour then breezes by some of the modernist architecture of the Government Quarter and on to the glass-and-steel Hauptbahnhof (train station), where—if you booked the evening cruise and it's sunny—you'll see crowds enjoying the sunshine, music, and drinks at the **Capital Beach Bar** (see p. 168). The boat continues to the **Tiergarten** (see pp. 98–99), before puttering pleasantly back to the starting point.

Burgstrasse 27 • www.bwsg-berlin.de • 030 65 13 41 5 • €€–€€€ • Closed early Nov.–end March • S-Bahn: Hackescher Markt

■ BEST KAYAK TOUR
Kayak Berlin Tours run several types of paddling tour through the city, including Night Tours, Stand Up Paddling Tours, and one in Potsdam. They also rent out equipment.

www.kajakberlintours.de • 030 99 54 80 18 • €€€€€

Cruising past the Hauptbahnhof, with Spreebogenpark in the foreground

■ Best Riverside Club

Berghain, in Berlin's east, might be the most famous club in town, but **Watergate** in the Kreuzberg neighborhood is certainly one of the best-looking. Party into the early hours in the club's main room, with glitzy LED ceiling and big-name house and techno DJs. To chill out, head straight for the outdoor terrace where you can enjoy a drink while looking out across the Spree River and views of **Oberbaumbrücke** (see p. 90).

Falckensteinstrasse 49 • www.water-gate.de • 030 61 28 03 94 • €€ • Closed Mon. • U-Bahn: Schlesisches Tor

■ Best Riverside Dining

Set on a moored Dutch sailing boat on a section of the Spree River in the Kreuzberg neighborhood, **Van Loon** (*Carl-Herz-Ufer, 030 69 26 29 3, €€*) is a charming spot for riverside drinks, a leisurely breakfast, or an al fresco dinner. For something more upscale, try the **Grill Royal** (*Friedrichstrasse 105b, 030 28 87 92 88, €€€€€*), a high-end steakhouse near Museumsinsel. It's popular with a well-heeled crowd and has a pleasant outdoor terrace that looks out over the Bode-Museum and the Spree River.

The giant Molecule Man sculpture rising from the Spree River

■ BEST RIVERSIDE VIEW

One of the city's most handsome bridges, the **Oberbaumbrücke** also has an illustrious history. Linking Kreuzberg and Friedrichshain across the Spree River, the bridge began life as a timber bridge in 1724, became a Cold War landmark during Berlin's division, and has starred in Hollywood movies like *The Bourne Supremacy*. Today, the bridge's arches and pseudo-medieval turrets offer great views along the Spree River in both directions.

Intersection of Warschauer Strasse and Mühlenstrasse • U-Bahn: Schlesisches Tor

■ BEST RIVERSIDE STATUE

It's hard to miss **Molecule Man**—the iconic 98-foot-tall (30 m) aluminum landmark by American sculptor Jonathan Borofsky—in Berlin's east. Three figures lean toward each other as if for mutual support, providing a symbol of togetherness for the reunited city.

An den Treptowers 1 • S-Bahn: Treptower Park

■ BEST RIVERSIDE ACCOMMODATIONS

There are great options for an overnight stay on the water. The most fun is the **Eastern Comfort**

Hostelboat (*Mühlenstrasse 73*, *www.eastern-comfort.com, 030 66 76 38 06, €–€€*), which offers simple single, double, and four-person cabins and a basic breakfast. It's located right next to the **East Side Gallery** (see p. 129) and the Oberbaumbrücke.

■ BEST RIVERSIDE FLEA MARKET
Every two weeks, on a Sunday morning, the section of the Maybachufer that lines the Landwehrkanal in the Kreuzkölln district comes alive with the buzzy **Nowkölln Flowmarkt** (*www.nowkoelln.de*), a flea market that sells secondhand wares and design objects

from local and international creatives. The market alway draws a youthful, happening crowd.

■ BEST BEACH BAR & POOL
The **Badeschiff** swimming pool is built from a recycled cargo container and floats right in the Spree River in Berlin's east. Conceived by local artist Susanne Lorenz, it's part of the sprawling Arena complex, which also features a nightclub, open-air bar, and sunbathing area. The venue has a beach with its own bar during summer.

Eichenstrasse 4 • www.arena-berlin.de • 030 53 32 03 0 • €€ • U-Bahn: Schlesisches Tor

Twilight on the banks of the Spree River, overlooking the Badeschiff

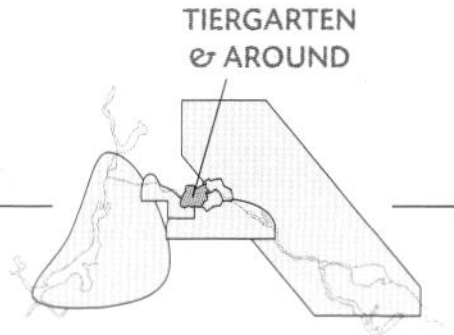

Tiergarten & Around

Dominated by the park from which it takes its name, this neighborhood has a unique—and particularly verdant—character. The Tiergarten itself is dissected by the majestic, tree-lined Strasse des 17. Juni.

A number of significant cultural venues flank the park, including the Neue Nationalgalerie, the Berliner Philharmonie, and the Bauhaus-Archiv to the south and the Haus der Kulturen der Welt (House of World Cultures) to the north, each designed by a leading architect of the 20th century. The buildings epitomize modern European architecture and—with contents that range from paintings by the old masters to seminal works from the Bauhaus movement—they contribute to this area's reputation as one of Berlin's primary cultural hubs.

◀ A number of pretty bridges cross the waterways that converge at Tiergarten See in the southern section of the park.

Tiergarten & Around

*This leisurely stroll in historic hunting grounds is bracketed by
the best of west Berlin's architectural and cultural sights.*

4 **Tiergarten** (see pp. 98–99)
Hofjägerallee will take you to
the Victory Column for great
views across the park. Explore
any one of the several walking
trails, before crossing Strasse
des 17. Juni on the way to the
park's northernmost flank.

5 **Haus der Kulturen der Welt** (see p. 99) Admire
the exterior of this building—dubbed the "pregnant
oyster" owing to its idiosyncratic shape— before
stepping inside for a wide range of events, concerts,
and exhibits from around the world.

0   200 meters
0   200 yards

Bellevue Ⓢ   LÜNEBURGER

PAULSTRASSE   STRASSE

ALTONAER STRASSE

Ⓤ Hansaplatz

Spree

**SCHLOSSPARK
BELLEVUE**

Schloss
Bellevue

SPREEWEG

To Tiergarten
← S-Bahn

STRASSE DES 17. JUNI

Tiergarten ❹   Siegessäule   **TIERGARTEN**

GROSSER
STERN

GROSSER STERNALLEE

FASANERIE-
ALLEE

HOFJÄGERALLEE

GROSSER

Neuer
See

LICHTENSTEIN-
ALLEE

WEG

RAUCH-
STRASSE

STULERSTR.

KLINGELHOFERSTR.

DIPLOMATENVIERTE

HIROSHIMA-
STRASSE

**Bauhaus-
Archiv** ❸

LÜTZOWUFER

To Nollendorfplatz

**TIERGARTEN & AROUND DISTANCE: 2.5 MILES (4 KM)
TIME: APPROX. 8 HOURS U-BAHN START: POTSDAMER PLATZ**

1 **Gemäldegalerie** (see pp. 100–101)
View the esteemed collection of European artworks spanning 500 years at Berlin's Picture Gallery—one of several highlights at the city's Kulturforum. You'll see the Neue Nationalgalerie across the square. Stroll south and then east past Matthäuskirche to reach it.

2 **Neue Nationalgalerie**
(see pp. 96–97) This celebrated example of Bauhaus architecture, another gem at the Kulturforum, contains an array of masterpieces from the 20th century. Walk west along the Landwehrkanal on Reichpietschufer and then on Von-der-Heydt-Strasse to Klingelhöferstrasse.

3 **Bauhaus-Archiv** (see p. 97) Inside the wavy-roofed building of the Bauhaus Archive you'll find exhibits from the seminal movement's leading designers, as well as an associated library. Head north on Klingelhöferstrasse and into the Tiergarten.

Gemäldegalerie

1 See pp. 100–101.

Matthäikirchplatz 4–6 • www.smb.museum • 030 26 64 24 24 2 • €€ (includes audioguide) • Closed Mon., Dec. 24, 31 • S-Bahn/U-Bahn: Potsdamer Platz

Neue Nationalgalerie

2 Known popularly as Berlin's "temple of light and glass," the New National Gallery boasts 54,000 square feet (5,000 sq m) of exhibition space. Its modern, clean-lined exterior—designed by Bauhaus affiliate Ludwig Mies van der Rohe—houses an extensive collection of European paintings and sculptures from the 19th century to the 1960s. The collection is displayed on a rotating basis across two vast floors and always includes works from major artists, including Pablo Picasso, Salvador Dalí, and Paul Klee. On permanent display are the works of Die Brücke (The Bridge) movement, a

Seminal works of 20th-century European art are on display at the Neue Nationalgalerie.

group of German Expressionists, formed in nearby Dresden, that included Karl Schmidt-Rottluff, Erich Heckel, and Ernst Ludwig Kirchner. Don't miss Kirchner's "Potsdamer Platz," depicting the square as it was in 1914, before it was bombed in World War II.

Potsdamer Strasse 50 • www.smb.museum • 030 26 64 24 24 2 • €€ • Closed Mon., Dec. 24, 31 • S-Bahn/U-Bahn: Potsdamer Platz

Bauhaus-Archiv

3 Housed in a somewhat idiosyncratic building featuring a flotilla-shaped roof (designed by Bauhaus founder Walter Gropius), this museum is one of the best places in the world to get a sense of the breadth and depth of the Bauhaus movement. The exhibition space houses around one-third of the museum's collection at a time, presenting works from students and luminaries alike. Bauhaus furnishings are well represented—you'll see classics like Wilhelm Wagenfeld's lamp and Marcel Breuer's Wassily chair, as well as some beautifully minimal armchairs and desks from Mies van der Rohe.

Other rooms contain paintings by the likes of Josef Albers and Paul Klee, and show how the movement's activities extended into wallpaper design and chess sets (don't miss Josef Hartwig's oak, maple, and pear set, with each piece designed to reflect the moves it makes in the game). Larger items include a curvaceous coffee bar, designed for the 1930 Werkbund Exhibition in Paris, and models of several architectural projects. The adjoining archive and library contain 26,000 books as well as manuscripts, letters, and a variety of Bauhaus-related publications.

Klingelhöferstrasse 14 • www.bauhaus.de • 030 25 40 02 0 • €€ (includes audioguide) • Closed Tues. and Dec. 24 • U-Bahn: Nollendorfplatz

GOOD **EATS**

■ **EDD'S**
This family-run restaurant serves some of the best Thai food in town, in an elegant wood-and-plant interior. **Lützowstrasse 81, 030 21 55 29 4, €€**

■ **FACIL**
This sophisticated Michelin-starred restaurant, set in the Mandala Hotel, is run by celebrated chef Michael Kempf. As well as high-end food (with an emphasis on fish), it offers splendid views from its fifth-floor dining room. **Potsdamer Strasse 3, 030 59 00 51 23 4, €€€**

■ **TEEHAUS IM ENGLISCHEN GARTEN**
A romantic, lakeside restaurant in the Tiergarten whose bistro-style dishes include soups, stews, and burgers. **Altonaer Strasse 2, 49 30 39 48 04 00, €€**

TIERGARTEN & AROUND

This Tiergarten statue depicts a family of lions, the lioness wounded by an arrow.

Tiergarten

4 The former hunting ground of the Great Elector Friedrich Wilhelm (1620–1688), the Tiergarten (Animal Garden) is one of Berlin's largest green spaces. Spanning more than 500 acres (200 ha), these green lungs contain almost 16 miles (25 km) of footpaths skirting a variety of lakes and ponds, gardens, flower beds, and meadows. Locals come here to jog, sunbathe, and play Frisbee, and there is a wide choice of picnic and barbecue spots, cafés, and beer gardens in which to while away the afternoon.

At the heart of the park—halfway along its main axis, Strasse des 17. Juni—stands the **Siegessäule** (*Grosser Stern 1, 030 39 12 96 1, €*). This column, topped in 1864 with a gilded statue of the winged goddess of victory, was erected in celebration of Prussian military success against the Danes. Climb the stairs to a platform near the top for views over the leafy park and the city beyond. North of here lies the elegant **Schloss Bellevue,** built in 1786 for the Prussian Prince August Ferdinand and now the official residence of the German president. At the eastern end of Strasse des 17. Juni stands the **Sowjetisches Ehrenmal** (Soviet Memorial), an immense bronze statue of a soldier on a marble plinth. It was built to commemorate Soviet victory over the Nazis during the Battle of Berlin (May 1945). The T-34 tanks that flank the monument are said to be the very ones that first fought their way into the city.

Strasse des 17. Juni • S-Bahn: Tiergarten

Haus der Kulturen der Welt

5 Located on the Spree River to the north of the Tiergarten, the House of World Cultures—with its dramatically sweeping roof and curvaceous facade—is fronted by an equally striking bronze sculpture, "**Large Divided Oval: Butterfly**" by British sculptor Henry Moore. Originally designed as a congress hall in 1957 and used specifically for international conferences and events, the building was a gift from the United States and symbolized the freedom of West Berlin (John F. Kennedy spoke here during his famed 1963 visit). Explore the expansive interior to find an auditorium, an exhibition hall, a roof terrace, and a number of smaller areas for concerts and theater projects. These spaces are used for themed events, exhibitions, festivals, lectures, and concerts—many with free admission—that focus on the culture and society of non-European nations. Recent programs have centered on subjects as diverse as forensic science, Korean cinema, and democracy in South Africa. The center also has a diverse musical program, with up to three concerts in an evening. Time your visit to coincide with one of these (*from 7 p.m.;* check the website for details).

John-Foster-Dulles-Allee 10 • www.hkw.de • 030 39 78 70 • €–€€€ • Closed Tues. (exhibitions only) • U-Bahn: Bundestag

SAVVY **TRAVELER**

If you are visiting Berlin in the summer, time your walk in the Tiergarten to coincide with a free concert at the **Teehaus im Englischen Garten** (Teahouse in the English Garden; see sidebar p. 97). Live music from blues and jazz to swing and soul fills the air on weekends at 4 p.m. and 7 p.m. from June through September.

TIERGARTEN & AROUND

Gemäldegalerie

The works of Brueghel, Dürer, Rubens, Rembrandt, and more jostle for wall space at Berlin's Picture Gallery.

Early works include Pieter Brueghel the Younger's "Carrying the Cross" (ca 1606).

With more than 1,000 works on view at a time—about half of those available—this collection of old masters constitutes one of the finest in Europe. It includes portraits, genre paintings, decorative panels, interiors, landscapes, and still lifes. Among the works are a number amassed by both the Great Elector Friedrich Wilhelm and Frederick the Great. The German and Dutch masterpieces from the 15th to the 17th centuries, and Italian collections from the 13th to the 16th centuries are particularly impressive.

TIERGARTEN & AROUND

WANDELHALLE

The rooms in this gallery are arranged around a vast central foyer—the Wandelhalle—and are organized geographically as well as chronologically. They follow a quirky numbering system for which there is no apparent explanation—some rooms have Roman numerals, while others use Arabic. At the center of the Wandelhalle, described as a meditation hall *(Ort der Ruhe und Besinnung)*, is a fountain installation by American artist Walter De Maria.

GERMAN AND FLEMISH WORKS

Rooms dedicated to German and Flemish works boast masterpieces that include **"Portrait of a Young Venetian Woman"** (1506) by Albrecht Dürer (Room 2); **"Altar with the Last Judgment"** (1524) by Lucas Cranach (Room III); **"Dutch Sayings"** (1559) by Pieter Brueghel the Elder (Room 7); and 16 Rembrandts, including a compelling self-portrait from 1634 (Room X).

ITALIAN WORKS

Key highlights in the Italian Renaissance section include no fewer than five different Madonnas by

SAVVY **TRAVELER**

Be aware that, beginning in 2015, there are plans to move this collection to the **Bode-Museum** on **Museumsinsel** (see sidebar p. 75). Although this may take several years, there is every chance that parts of the collection may already have been relocated by the time of your visit.

Raphael (Room 29). Collectively, they demonstrate the painter's progression in confidence and style from his early work to his time in Florence. Additional Italian masterpieces include such famous works as Caravaggio's **"Love Conquers All"** (1602), Botticelli's **"Portrait of a Lady"** (1460–1465), and Correggio's **"Leda and the Swan"** (ca 1530), the famous depiction of the popular Greek myth, in which the god Zeus takes the form of a swan in order to seduce a young woman.

A CLOSER LOOK

For a detailed study of some of the more prominent paintings on display, you'll find a **digital gallery** with computer guides on the lower floor (accessed by stairs from Room XV).

Matthäikirchplatz 4–6 • www.smb.museum • 030 26 64 24 24 2 • €€ (includes free audioguide in English) • Closed Mon., Dec. 24, and 31 • S-Bahn/U-Bahn: Potsdamer Platz

TIERGARTEN & AROUND

Cultural Capital

With the fall of the wall, newly united Berlin became Germany's cultural as well as governmental capital. Today, it offers classical events alongside a thriving avant-garde scene. Like so much in Berlin, the city's cultural identity is rooted in the events of the last 100 years—from the decadence of the 1920s' arts scene to the legacy of the divided city to its current role as national capital.

The Berlin International Film Festival draws audiences approaching half a million and previews as many as 400 films. Opposite: Concertgoers enjoy a classical concert at Berlin's Philharmonie.

Cultural Divisions

In divided Berlin, both sides used culture as a form of propaganda. East Berlin offered world-class opera and concerts with tickets one-tenth the price of those in New York and London. In West Berlin, the glamorous **Berlinale** (Berlin International Film Festival; *www.berlinale.de*) was launched in 1951 and remains a mainstay of the city's cultural calendar. A move in the 1960s to create a new cultural hub in a bombed-out area of West Berlin near the wall resulted in the **Kulturforum** (*www.kulturforum-berlin.com*) with its showpiece architecture by Mies van der Rohe and Hans Scharoun. It includes museums, libraries, and the **Berliner Philharmonie** (*Herbert-von-Karajan-Strasse 1, www.berliner-philharmoniker.de, 030 25 48 80*), Berlin's premier venue for classical music.

Arts at the Cutting Edge

The Berlin tradition of artistic experimentation that emerged after World War I (see pp. 64–67) continues thanks in part to the city's many vacant industrial buildings, which give dancers, artists, and

TIERGARTEN & AROUND

creative types the space to create large-scale works. For example, **Radialsystem V** *(Holzmarktstrasse 33, www.radialsystem.de, 030 28 87 88 50)* is housed in a converted water-pumping station on the banks of the Spree River, and provides innovative performances, family-friendly events, and a relaxing riverside terrace.

On Stage

Unsurprisingly in the city that inspired Bertolt Brecht, theater is important to Berlin's cultural life. The **Deutches Theater** *(Schumannstrasse 13a, www.deutschestheater.de, 030 28 44 12 25)* has occupied the same building since 1883, while the **English Theatre Berlin** *(Fidicinstrasse 40, www .etberlin.de, 030 69 35 692)* works in English, for them the lingua franca of the 21st century.

BERLIN **ON CELLULOID**

Few capital cities have inspired the film industry as much as Berlin has. Explore the city on the silver screen with **The Blue Angel** (1930) starring Marlene Dietrich (see p. 65), Billy Wilder's **One, Two, Three** (1961), Wim Wenders's **Wings of Desire** (1987), Tom Tykwer's **Run Lola Run** (1998), and Wolfgang Becker's **Good Bye, Lenin!** (2003).

TIERGARTEN & AROUND

City Parks

Berlin is one of Europe's greenest cities, with a wealth of public spaces available for strolling, sunbathing, and sports. Many parks share characteristics with the city's largest—the Tiergarten (see pp. 98–99)—and are home to a number of significant memorials, museums, and more.

■ SPREEBOGENPARK

This newly landscaped park nestles into a bend in the Spree River in the northwestern corner of the Tiergarten neighborhood. Sandwiched between two bridges, the park has split-level walkways planted with boxwood and riverside grasses. They provide great views of central Berlin and direct access to the waterfront.

Spreebogenpark • U-Bahn: Bundestag

■ MONBIJOUPARK

Once the grounds of Monbijou Palace, this small park located opposite **Museumsinsel** (see pp. 70–91) is perfectly located for taking a break from sightseeing. It's especially good for kids, thanks to the two pools (swimming and paddling) and an ice-cream kiosk. There are also benches and trees for shade.

Monbijoustrasse 3 • S-Bahn: Hackescher Markt

■ TEMPELHOFER PARK

Bridging the Schöneberg and Kreuzberg neighborhoods, this defunct airport—expanded into its current format by the Nazis—was proclaimed a public space in 2010. The former runway is a particularly popular spot for kite-surfing, cycling, and in-line skating. Among the park's diverse attractions you'll find everything from a **Shaolin temple** and community gardens to sculptures by local artists and official grilling areas. Parts of the former **Flughafen** (airport buildings) can also be accessed by several different guided tours (see website for details) and are sometimes used for major events, such as the annual **Berlinale** (see pp. 102–103) and the **Bread and Butter** fashion show (see p. 134).

Tempelhofer Damm 1 • wwwtempelhoferfreiheit .de • 30 200 03 74-00 • S-Bahn/U-Bahn: Tempelhof

Kite-surfing on the former runway at Tempelhofer Park

■ MAUERPARK

Formerly the site of the Berlin Wall and its associated Death Strip, Wall Park in Berlin's east became a community park in the early 1990s. Flanked to the east by Friedrich-Ludwig-Jahn Sports Stadium (remnants of the former wall can still be seen at the top of the embankment here), the park occupies a special place in the hearts of Berliners. A neighboring area hosts a flea market on Sundays (see p. 153) and an amphitheater that is home to popular karaoke sessions in summer (see p. 171).

Gleimstrasse 55 • U-Bahn: Bernauer Strasse

■ TREPTOWER PARK

Dominated by the 24-acre (10 ha) **Soviet Memorial** that commemorates the death of the 20,000 Russians who died in the Battle of Berlin, Treptower Park in Berlin's east also offers a promenade along the Spree River, leafy woods, and a pleasant **Karpfenteich** ("carp pond"). You can also visit the **Archenhold-Sternwarte** observatory (*Alt-Treptow 1, www.sdtb.de, 030 53 60 63 71 9, €, closed Mon.–Tues.*), where Einstein gave his first public lecture on his theory of relativity.

Alt-Treptow • S-Bahn: Treptower Park

CHARLOTTENBURG

Charlottenburg

Historically one of Berlin's wealthier neighborhoods, Charlottenburg evolved into a major cultural hub during the Weimar era, brimming with bars, galleries, department stores, and cabarets. During the years of division, the area maintained its commercial feel, and remains one of the best parts of the city for shopping, as well as sightseeing. Its main street, Kurfürstendamm (or Ku'damm for short), is Berlin's answer to the Champs-Elysées in Paris and London's Oxford Street. This large-scale, leafy boulevard is lined with leading fashion stores and restaurants, while its elegant side streets are home to clusters of antique dealers, independent boutiques, and more. Nearby sights include Berlin's prestigious royal residence, Schloss Charlottenburg—from which the neighborhood takes its name—the war-torn tower of Kaiser Wilhelm Memorial Church, and the deeply thought-provoking Käthe-Kollwitz-Museum.

CHARLOTTENBURG

◐ **The lavish interior of the Golden Gallery at Schloss Charlottenburg**

NEIGHBORHOOD **WALK**

❶ Schloss Charlottenburg (see pp. 114–117) **Allow three hours to explore the many rooms and wonderful gardens of this former royal residence. Walk south on Kaiser-Friedrich-Strasse to Adenauerplatz.**

SCHLOSSGARTEN
CHARLOTTENBURG

Mausoleum

To the
Belvedere

**Schloss
Charlottenburg**

Neuer
Pavillon

Altes Schloss
❶
Neuer Flügel

Orangerie

Gipsformerei
SPANDAUER DAMM

KLAUSENERPLATZ

Westend

OTTO-SUHR ALLEE

Richard-Ⓤ
Wagner-Platz

DANCKELMANNSTRASSE

SCHLOSSSTRASSE

KAISER-FRIEDRICH-STRASSE

SCHUSTEHRUS-
PARK

CHARLOTTENBURG

ZILLESTRASSE

CAUERSTRASSE

LEIBNIZSTRASSE

SOPHIE-
CHARLOTTE-
PLATZ

BISMARCKSTRASSE
Bismarckstrasse Ⓤ

Ⓤ Deutsche
Oper

SCHILLERSTRASSE

Ⓤ Sophie-
Charlotte-
Platz

CHARLOTTENBURG

❷ Kurfürstendamm
(see pp. 110–111)
Discover the myriad shops, galleries, and museums on both sides of this famous and eternally busy boulevard. Halfway along, head south on Fasanenstrasse.

| 0 | 500 meters |
| 0 | 500 yards |

❸ Käthe-Kollwitz-Museum
(see p. 111) This museum provides an insight into the pacifist artist's work and life. Return to Ku'damm and continue east to Breitscheidplatz.

CHARLOTTENBURG DISTANCE: 3.5 MILES (5.6 KM) TIME: APPROX. 10 HOURS U-BAHN START: RICHARD-WAGNER-PLATZ

Charlottenburg

*Combine the riches of Prussian luxury with a good
shopping spree in Berlin's royal neighborhood.*

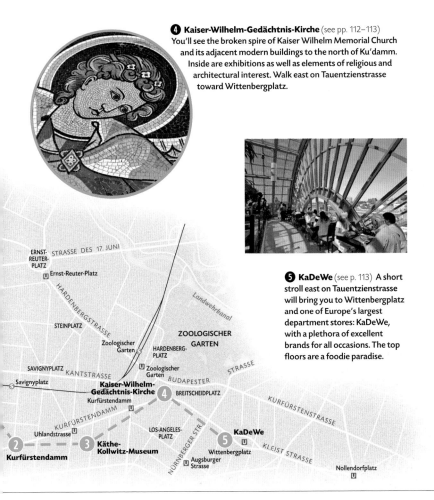

4 **Kaiser-Wilhelm-Gedächtnis-Kirche** (see pp. 112–113)
You'll see the broken spire of Kaiser Wilhelm Memorial Church
and its adjacent modern buildings to the north of Ku'damm.
Inside are exhibitions as well as elements of religious and
architectural interest. Walk east on Tauentzienstrasse
toward Wittenbergplatz.

5 **KaDeWe** (see p. 113) A short
stroll east on Tauentzienstrasse
will bring you to Wittenbergplatz
and one of Europe's largest
department stores: KaDeWe,
with a plethora of excellent
brands for all occasions. The top
floors are a foodie paradise.

Schloss Charlottenburg

1 See pp. 114–117.

Spandauer Damm 10–22 • www.spsg.de • 030 32 09 10 • €–€€€€ (includes free audioguide) • Closed Mon. • U-Bahn: Richard-Wagner-Platz

Kurfürstendamm

2 Charlottenburg's main boulevard, Kurfürstendamm, is known as Ku'damm for short and offers a mix of high-end fashion boutiques, chain stores, and classy restaurants. The most exclusive stores lie at the western end, where you'll find the likes of **Chanel** *(No. 188)*, **Yves Saint Laurent** *(No. 52)*, and **Luis Vuitton** *(No. 57)* interspersed with chic boutiques that include men's haute couture store **Harveys Herrenmode** *(No. 56, www.harveys-berlin .de, 030 88 33 80 3)*, ladies emporium **Veronica Pohle** *(No. 64, 030 88 33 73 1)*, and quality shoe store **Budapester Schuhe** *(No. 199, www.budapester.eu, 030 88 62 42 06)*.

Each gallery at the Story of Berlin has a different theme. Here, the subject is "Military."

For a break from shopping, head to the **Story of Berlin** (*Nos. 207–208, www.story-of-berlin .de, 030 88 72 01 00, €€€*). Eight centuries of Berlin's history are brought to life via photos, films, interactive exhibits, and a free tour of an atomic bomb shelter (*given in English at 12 p.m., 2 p.m., 4 p.m., and 6 p.m.*). Stroll into Ku'damm's eastern environs for medium-priced international fashion chains and sport brands, as well as around 70 shops located in the **Europa-Center** (*Breitscheidplatz, www.europa-center-berlin.de*).

East-west axis between Joachim-Friedrich-Strasse in the west and Tauentzienstrasse in the east • U-Bahn: Adenauer Platz

Käthe-Kollwitz-Museum

3 Housed in a handsome 19th-century villa, this museum hosts an extensive collection of works by one of Berlin's most famous 20th-century female artists. With charcoal sketches, woodcuts, lithographs, and sculptures, the permanent exhibition reflects Kollwitz's status as a lifelong pacifist dedicated to campaigning against war and suffering, especially for women and children. The first floor begins with early political works such as "A Weavers Uprising" (1893–1897) and "Peasants' War" (1902–1908). Works on the second and third floors include a striking collection of posters created in 1924 for International Workers Aid, bearing potent titles such as "Germany's Children Are Starving!," "Bread!," and "Never Again War!" Perhaps the most poignant though, are the sketches and sculptures that Kollwitz created during the outbreak of World War I, to which she lost a son. Their heartbreaking titles— "Widowed Orphans," "Killed in Action," and "Survivors"—say it all.

Fasanenstrasse 24 • www.kaethe-kollwitz.de • 030 88 25 21 0 • €€ • U-Bahn: Uhlandstrasse

GOOD **EATS**

■ **BIER'S KU'DAMM**
If you are tempted to try currywurst, try it here, at one of the only spots in the city that sells the famed fast food as well as champagne. **Ku'damm 195, 030 88 18 94 2, €**

■ **CAFÉ IM LITERATURHAUS**
Enjoy lunch, dinner, or just *Kaffee und Kuchen* at this elegant café in a pleasant villa next to the Käthe-Kollwitz-Museum. If it's sunny, grab a seat in the garden. **Fasanenstrasse 23, 030 88 25 41 4, €€**

■ **PARIS BAR**
A central hub for the former West Berlin's prolific art scene until the wall fell, there's still something enjoyably bohemian about the Paris Bar and its reliable French menu. **Kantstrasse 152, 030 31 38 05 2, €€**

CHARLOTTENBURG

The Kaiser-Wilhelm-Gedächtnis-Kirche was built to glorify the first emperor of the unified Germany.

Kaiser-Wilhelm-Gedächtnis-Kirche

4 Located at the eastern end of **Ku'damm** (see pp. 110–111), what remains of the late 19th-century Kaiser Wilhelm Memorial Church is one of west Berlin's most dramatic sights. All but destroyed during World War II, the base of the old spire (deliberately left bomb-damaged) and vestibule of the original church now serve as a **Hall of Remembrance.** Here, you'll find display panels documenting the church's history and its destruction, through photos, historical illustrations, artifacts, and objects that survived the bombing. A number of restored mosaics include one on the floor that depicts Archangel Michael fighting the dragon.

The modern buildings on this site were designed by celebrated German architect Egon Eiermann in the 1950s. They include the octagonal **Neue Kirche** and the **Neuer Turm** (New Church and Tower). Step into either and savor the impact made by the stained glass. There are 21,000 individual panes—almost all of them blue. Additional sights within the church include an aluminum baptismal font filled with marble pebbles and a dramatic mechanical organ. Look above the altar to see a sculpture of Christ made from tombac—a brasslike alloy of zinc and copper. See how it glows against the blue of the stained glass. On the northeastern wall are three artworks: Kurt Reuber's charcoal "Stalingrad Madonna," drawn in 1942 and placed here as a reminder of the deaths of hundreds of thousands of soldiers on both the German and Russian sides; a bronze plaque commemorating

CHARLOTTENBURG

Protestant martyrs under the Nazi regime (see if you can spot the 13th-century Spanish crucifix); and an icon of the Virgin Mary from Volgograd. An adjacent 174-foot (53 m) tower contains a belfry with six bronze bells that chime on the hour. The church holds music services on Saturdays (6 p.m.).

Breitscheidplatz • www.gedaechtniskirche-berlin
.de • 030 21 85 02 3 • U-Bahn: Kurfürstendamm

KaDeWe

⑤ Formally known as the Kaufhaus des Westens (Department Store of the West), but abbreviated to KaDeWe, this shopper's paradise is the largest of its kind in continental Europe. Expect the place to be busy—you'll be one of 180,000 visitors who come here daily.

Each of the store's eight floors is loosely arranged around a retail theme: first floor for beauty products and luxury goods, second floor for men, third for women, fourth for children, and so on. If you're a foodie, take an elevator straight to the seventh floor, where 30 gourmet counters serve everything from currywurst to imported Italian delicacies. The top floor also has a 1,000-seat, glass-fronted restaurant and winter garden with great views over the city.

Tauentzienstrasse 21–24 • www.kadewe.de
• 030 21 21 0 • U-Bahn: Wittenbergplatz

IN **THE KNOW**

Currywurst—Germany's answer to exotic fast food—originated in this neighborhood. The story goes that, in 1949, Charlottenburg sausage stand holder Herta Heuwer began playing around with sauces while waiting for customers to show up. Throwing curry powder and chili into tomato sauce, and blending it with a dash of Worcester sauce, Heuwer tried out her secret "Chillup" combination and it was an instant success. A plaque at Kantstrasse 101 commemorates the event.

Overlooking the central hall at KaDeWe. The store first opened its doors in 1907.

CHARLOTTENBURG

Schloss Charlottenburg

Experience the luxuries of life enjoyed by the royal inhabitants of this opulent Prussian palace.

The majestic facade of the Old Palace at Schloss Charlottenburg

Schloss Charlottenburg is the largest remaining royal residence in the German capital. Former residents of the Old Palace building include Queen Sophie Charlotte, second wife of Friedrich I, king of Prussia, in the early 1700s, and Friedrich II (Frederick the Great) in the 1750s. A visit to this site and its landscaped gardens—studded with flower beds, statues, and several notable buildings—provides a compelling insight into the courtly life of Brandenburg-Prussia from the baroque period right up until the early 20th century.

ALTES SCHLOSS

You access the Old Palace (€€€, *closed Mon.*) via the **Great Courtyard,** with its equestrian statue of Friedrich Wilhelm I, son of Friedrich I. Before entering the building, admire the monumental 165-foot (50 m) domed tower, added between 1710 and 1712, which can be seen for miles around.

The first room you enter displays photographs of how the palace looked directly after World War II—that is, largely devastated—and underlines how much of the opulence that follows is due to careful restoration. Only a smattering of the interiors, antiquities, and artworks scattered throughout the bedrooms, beauty rooms, studies, and audience chambers survived the bombings; the rest were drafted in from former Prussian palaces elsewhere, including the **Berliner Schloss** (see sidebar p. 119).

Among the many exquisite treasures on both floors are paintings and portraits of the palace's previous inhabitants and their royal relatives and esteemed friends. Some rooms boast entire walls of damask and original writing desks, others have beautiful tapestries and French-style ceiling frescoes. One room even has an original white harpsichord that was played by Sophie Charlotte.

SAVVY **TRAVELER**

Schloss Charlottenburg is best seen on a self-guided tour. Expect to spend at least three hours here. While the palace gardens are free to enter, each of the individual buildings has a separate entrance fee. Purchase a day card (€€€€) that allows you access to all of the buildings. Start at the Altes Schloss and the Neuer Flügel, then see how much time you have left for the other sights.

Don't miss the dazzling **Porzellankabinett** (Porcelain Cabinet; Room 95), one of the oldest and largest of its kind in Germany, which contains some 2,700 items of exquisite chinoiserie, and the **Kronschatz** (Crown Jewels; Room 230), including the golden crowns of Friedrich I and Sophie Charlotte.

The palace's west wing features the **Grosse Orangerie** (Great Orangerie). Mainly used for cultural events and classical concerts today, this extension was originally to be mirrored on the eastern side of the building, but Frederick the Great had other plans.

NEUER FLÜGEL

In place of the proposed orangerie, Frederick the Great added a rococo New Wing (€€, *closed Tues.*) to the eastern side of the Altes Schloss. The first section of the building was finished in 1742, with rooms designed by royal architect Georg Wenzeslaus von Knobelsdorff, while the upper floor was designed mainly by Johann August Nahl. Most of the highlights are, in fact, upstairs. They include—to the left at the top of the stairs—the flamboyant banqueting hall, called the **Weisser Saal** (White Hall). Beyond that is the **Goldene Galerie** (Golden Gallery), a 138-foot-long (42 m) ballroom with mesmerizing aquamarine walls. Within the king's

Exquisite stuccoed walls with gilt decoration at Schloss Charlottenburg

private chambers is an important rococo painting by Antoine Watteau, **"Einschiffung nach Cythera"** ("Pilgrimage to Cythera"), ca 1718.

■ NEUER PAVILLON

Just beyond the Neuer Flügel is the New Pavilion *(030 32 09 10, €€, closed Mon.).* Built by Prussian architect Karl Friedrich Schinkel in 1825 as a summer retreat for King Friedrich Wilhelm III, this charming Italianate villa was reconstructed in 1970. The former rooms, arranged on two stories around an elegant staircase, exhibit paintings, furniture, artworks, and porcelain from the "Schinkel era." Stop to admire romantic landscapes by Schinkel himself—a gifted painter as well as architect—and his contemporaries Caspar David Friedrich, Karl Blechen, and Eduard Gärtner.

■ SCHLOSSGARTEN

The Palace Gardens are one of the venue's real highlights. Reflecting different periods of the palace's history, the section directly behind the **Altes Schloss** (see p. 115) follows the original, geometric planting plan (designed after the French model), while the rest retains the late 18th- and early 19th-century restyling, which follows the less formal English model.

The immaculately tended baroque-style Schlossgarten

Heading north through the gardens, you'll first come across the neoclassical **Mausoleum** *(€, closed Jan.–March and Nov.–Dec.)*, built in 1810 to house the tomb of Queen Luise. You'll also find the marble sarcophagi of other members of the royal family here, such as Queen Luise's husband, King Friedrich Wilhelm III, and Kaiser Wilhelm I and his wife Augusta.

Still heading north, the pretty, three-story **Belvedere** *(€, closed Jan.– March and Nov.–Dec.)* sits on the banks of the Spree River. Designed by Carl Gotthard Langhans, architect of the **Brandenburger Tor** (see p. 54), the belvedere was initially conceived as a teahouse for King Friedrich Wilhelm II. The somewhat unexpected contents of the building include a world-renowned collection of porcelain—wall fittings, decorative vases, statuettes, dinner services, and tea sets of various Prussian kings—all made by Berlin's royal manufacturer KPM (Königliche Porzellan-Manufaktur, or the Royal Porcelain Manfacturers).

Spandauer Damm 10–22 • www.spsg.de • 030 32 09 10 • €–€€€€ (includes free audioguide) • Closed Mon. • U-Bahn: Richard-Wagner-Platz

Royal City

Berlin's great royal age began in 1701, when Friedrich III, Duke of Prussia, had himself crowned Friedrich I, King of Prussia. He brought together five towns— Berlin, Cölln, Friedrichswerder, Dorotheenstadt, and Friedrichstadt—to form the capital and royal residence of Berlin. From that time until the end of the monarchy in 1918, Berlin benefited from a number of royal patrons.

CHARLOTTENBURG

**A champion of the Enlightenment, Frederick the Great studied music and French literature, and even wrote and composed several works himself.
Opposite: Prinz-Heinrich-Palais at the Forum Fridericianum in a lithograph by W. Loeillot, ca 1840**

Frederick's Forum

Friedrich I's grandson, Friedrich II (Frederick the Great, 1740–1786), shaped the Berlin cityscape that we see today. One of his first projects, started in 1741, was the Forum Fridericianum, designed by architect Georg Wenzeslaus von Knobelsdorff in a mix of architectural styles (neoclassical, baroque, rococo) as a new scientific center and artistic focal point for the Prussian Kingdom. Built around the former Opernplatz (today's **Bebelplatz;** see p. 59) the Forum included the Staatsoper, St. Hedwig's Cathedral, the Zeughaus, Kronprinzenpalais, Opernpalais, and Prinz-Heinrich-Palais.

Art and Science

The **Altes Museum** (see sidebar p. 75), the first museum built in Berlin, was constructed in 1830 by Karl Friedrich Schinkel. But it was romanticist Friedrich Wilhelm IV (1840–1848) who dedicated the **Museumsinsel,** originally a residential area, to "art and science" in 1841. He personally commissioned the **Alte Nationalgalerie** and the **Neues Museum** (see pp. 82–85). All the important city architects— Schinkel, Langhans, Knobelsdorff, and Nering— were involved in the construction of the island.

The Last Kaiser

Wilhelm II (1888–1918) was famous for his conservative tastes and hatred of anything "modern." His favorite architect was Ernst von Ihne, and his major buildings include the neo-Romanesque **Kaiser-Wilhelm-Gedächtnis-Kirche** (see pp. 112–113). He also famously lined a Tiergarten path leading up to the **Siegessäule** (see p. 98) with bland statues of former kings—a move that was sarcastically dubbed the *"Puppenallee"* ("street of the dolls") by locals. Germany's defeat in World War I led to revolt against the monarchy and Kaiser Wilhelm II was Germany's last royal patron.

BERLINER SCHLOSS

The Prussian monarchy's winter residence, the **Berliner Schloss,** was first built on **Museumsinsel** in 1443. In 1950 it was destroyed by the GDR (DDR). A version of the original is currently being rebuilt at a cost of €590 million ($787 million). The German parliament has insisted that three of the palace's four facades should be rebuilt as well as Schlüter's entrance dome, although the interior will house exhibition halls, a library, restaurants, a theater, and an auditorium. The building is scheduled for completion in 2019. The temporary **Humboldt-Box** (see p. 24) offers a scale model and more information on the project.

CHARLOTTENBURG

Christmas Markets

With roots in the late Middle Ages, the German Christmas market has long been a fixture of the festive season. Throughout Advent, markets big and small switch on their fairy lights and fill the air with the enticing smells of cookies, sausages, and Glühwein. Dates vary year to year, so check websites for details.

■ SCHLOSS CHARLOTTENBURG

One of Berlin's most romantic markets takes place on the grounds of **Schloss Charlottenburg** (see pp. 114–117), where you'll find more than 150 stalls, many inside heated tents and elegant glass pagodas. On-site entertainment includes Ferris wheels, live music, choirs, and a children's market with its own carousel and petting zoo. The palace gardens are illuminated especially for the event.

Spandauer Damm • U-Bahn: Richard-Wagner-Platz

■ GENDARMENMARKT

Set between the beautiful domes of the **Deutscher Dom** and **Französischer Dom** on **Gendarmenmarkt** (see pp. 60–61) in the Unter den Linden neighborhood, this market offers a dizzying array of stalls and activities. Culinary delights are supplied by upmarket establishments such as **Galeries Lafayette** and **Lutter & Wegner,** as well as the usual crêpe and grill stalls. There are also lots of high-end artisanal gifts to buy and a weekend stage program (*€ entry*) hosting everything from fire artists to gospel singers.

Gendarmenmarkt • www.gendarmenmarkt berlin.de • U-Bahn: Hausvogteiplatz

■ OPERNPALAIS

Officially titled the Nostalgic Christmas Market, this event at the Opernpalais on Unter den Linden offers a program of live music, family activities, and an art exhibition. There are more than 150 stands selling everything from roast chestnuts to South Tyrolean specialties, fairground carousels for kids, and romantic carriage rides for adults.

Unter den Linden • U-Bahn: Hausvogteiplatz

Irresistible Christmas goodies at the Gendarmenmarkt

■ RIXDORFER WEIHNACHTSMARKT

Another unique experience can be found nestled in the heart of trendy Kreuzkölln on the fringes of the Kreuzberg neighborhood. Quaint at the best of times, with its medieval houses and cobbled streets, the small bohemian village of Rixdorf takes on an extra-nostalgic hue for three days at the beginning of December, with market stalls hawking handmade goods, local schnapps, special pony rides around the stables, and demonstrations by blacksmiths.

Richardplatz • U-Bahn: Karl-Marx-Strasse

■ LUCIA WEIHNACHTSMARKT
AT THE KULTURBRAUEREI

This Scandinavian-themed market takes place in the handsome cobbled courtyard of the **Kulturbrauerei** in Berlin's eastern district of Prenzlauer Berg (see p. 126). Named after the Nordic goddess of light, the market includes plenty of Nordic-themed stalls selling things like Norwegian punch, specialty chocolates, and designer housewares. There are plenty of food and gift stalls, kids' rides—and even a sauna.

Schönhauser Allee 36 • U-Bahn: Eberswalder Strasse

Berlin's East

Every city has its "east side," but Berlin's has the distinction of having also been the capital of an entirely different country for several decades. The erection of the Berlin Wall in 1961 meant that the city's eastern districts suddenly found themselves part of the GDR (DDR) until reunification in 1990. This half of the city subsequently developed in a distinctly different direction to its western counterpart, architecturally, socially, and politically.

The post-reunification frenzy of cultural and commercial activity in the former GDR (DDR) districts of Mitte, Prenzlauer Berg, and Friedrichshain resulted in rampant regeneration of Berlin's east. Today, the overriding character of this neighborhood is one of trendy residential areas defined by broad, cobbled streets, 19th-century housing, and a slew of upscale cafés, restaurants, and boutiques. Explore a little farther, however, and you'll find fascinating remnants of the area's communist past.

◗ **The redbrick turrets of Oberbaumbrücke rise above what's left of the Berlin Wall at the East Side Gallery.**

❶ Gedenkstätte Berliner Mauer
(see pp. 130–131) Visit Berlin's most poignant memorial to those who fell at the Berlin Wall. Walk east on Oderberger Strasse.

❷ Kulturbrauerei
(see p. 126) Explore the neighborhood's 19th-century industrial roots with a visit to this former brewery, now a cultural complex with shops, a cinema, and live music venues. Walk south on Knaackstrasse.

❸ Kollwitzplatz (see p. 127) Stop for lunch in or around handsome Kollwitzplatz. Walk southeast on Wörther Strasse, then Marienburger Strasse, and finally Hufelandstrasse to reach Am Friedrichshain.

**BERLIN'S EAST DISTANCE: 7 MILES (11.5 KM)
TIME: APPROX. 8 HOURS S-BAHN START: NORDBAHNHOF**

Berlin's East

Pretty residential streets and reminders of the Cold War define this tour of Berlin's eastern districts.

6 East Side Gallery (see p. 129) **Staying** on Mühlenstrasse, view the largest open-air gallery in the world. The vivid display of street art harks back to the fall of the Berlin Wall in 1989.

5 Karl-Marx-Allee (see p. 128) **Admire** the Soviet architecture of this monumental boulevard. Take the bus (no. 142) heading south on Andreasstrasse. Alight at Ostbahnhof for a short walk south to Mühlenstrasse.

4 Volkspark Friedrichshain (see p. 128) **Enter the park at** Virchowstrasse and explore its 128 acres (52 ha) with special areas for climbing, jogging, and skateboarding. Exit at Friedenstrasse and head south on Lichtenberger Strasse to Strausberger Platz.

Once a thriving brewery, the Kulturbrauerei is now a multivenue entertainment and culture center.

Gedenkstätte Berliner Mauer

1 See pp. 130–131.

Bernauer Strasse • www.berliner -mauer-gedenkstaette.de • 030 46 79 6 66 6 • Visitor Center closed Mon. • S-Bahn: Nordbahnhof

Kulturbrauerei

2 This red-and-yellow-brick complex once functioned as one of the most important breweries in Berlin. Dating back to 1842, the 6-acre (2.5 ha) site was refurbished during the 1990s into an entertainment and culture complex. Its various buildings are now occupied by an array of cafés, shops, restaurants, and clubs. In summer, its handsome cobbled courtyards host events like children's fairs and classical concerts. The popular **Nordic-themed Christmas Market** (Lucia Weihnachtsmarkt; see p. 121) takes place here in winter. On arrival, make for the permanent **"Alltag in der DDR"** exhibition ("Everyday in the GDR"; *Knaackstrasse 97, 030 46 77 77 90*), which displays original objects, documents, films, and audio recordings from the days of East Germany. Afterward, browse eco-furniture at **Green Living** (*030 80 61 48 00*) or grab some tasty tapas next door at **Queso y Jamon** (*030 44 03 39 27*). The brewery's former boiler house, the **Kesselhaus** is one of Berlin's rock venues and attracts an impressive lineup of bands that includes The Killers and Kaiser Chiefs. There are no contact details online, so drop by to see what's on during your stay.

Schönhauser Allee 36 • www.kulturbrauerei.de • U-Bahn: Eberswalder Strasse

BERLIN'S EAST

Kollwitzplatz

3 The beating heart of trendy Prenzlauer Berg, this vibrant square is named after celebrated artist and pacifist Käthe Kollwitz (1867–1945), who lived in the area at the turn of the 20th century. A haven for young families, the square has three separate playgrounds and a leafy park. It's surrounded on all sides by rows of refurbished 19th-century houses, whose ground floors contain numerous bars and cafés. There is barely any traffic, and you could happily stop for a drink while the children play. This is a great spot for a little laid-back shopping—a few stylish housewares from **Stilkeller am Kollwitzplatz** (*Knaackstrasse 47*) or überchic clothing from **M-45 Fashion Lounge** (*Kollwitzstrasse 93*). The square attracts a particularly buzzy crowd on Saturdays, when it hosts an organic farmers market (see p. 153).

Kollwitzplatz • U-Bahn: Eberswalder Strasse

IN **THE KNOW**

Prenzlauer Berg's standout landmark is the **Wasserturm** on Knaackstrasse. Known as Fat Hermann (Dicker Hermann) by locals, this brick water tower is Berlin's oldest (1877), having stored the area's supply until the 1950s. Today, it houses luxury apartments and stands in pretty landscaped gardens—a handy retreat should Kollwitzplatz feel overcrowded.

Children play at one of several fun playgrounds at the center of Kollwitzplatz.

GOOD **EATS**

■ **CAFÉ SCHÖNBRUNN**
Set in a former-GDR (DDR)
pavilion in Volkspark
Friedrichshain, this café serves
Austrian-Mediterranean cuisine.
**Am Schwanenteich im
Volkspark Friedrichshain, 030
45 30 56 52 5, €€**

■ **GUGELHOF**
This Kollwitzplatz favorite serves
food from the Alsace region,
including *Flammkuchen* (tarte
flambée). **Knaackstrasse 37,
030 44 29 22 9, €–€€**

■ **LA SOUP POPULAIRE**
Run by celebrity chef Tim Raue,
this restaurant serves modern
Berlin and Thai food. The
industrial interior of this former
brewery is reason enough to go.
**Prenzlauer Allee 242, 030 44
31 96 80, €€€€**

Volkspark Friedrichshain

4 The Friedrichshain People's Park is second
only in size to the Tiergarten (see pp. 98–99).
Focus your visit on two outstanding memorials
from the GDR (DDR) era. As you enter the park
you'll see the twin columns of the **Memorial to
Polish Soldiers and German Anti-Fascists,**
which celebrates the communist resistance
fighters who joined forces against National
Socialism. On leaving the park, on Friedenstrasse,
don't miss the **Memorial to the International
Brigades in the Spanish Civil War,** honoring
the communist volunteers who fought for the
Republic in the Spanish Civil War (1936–1939;
pictured p. 125). Stylistically, these sculptures
epitomize the socialist realism that pervaded all
communist culture during the Cold War years.

Am Friedrichshain 1 • www.visitberlin.de/de/ort/volkspark
-friedrichshain • U-Bahn: Strausberger Platz

Karl-Marx-Allee

5 Conceived by the GDR (DDR) as a flagship of postwar
Soviet architecture, 2-mile-long (3.2 km) Karl-Marx-Allee
was constructed during the 1950s and 1960s. Imposing, Soviet-
style apartment houses line the boulevard. Head straight for **Café
Moskau** *(No. 34)*, a treasure trove of Soviet art and sculpture—
from its modernist structure to the socialist-realist mosaic gracing
its facade and the *Sputnik* model zooming into the sky above it.
Across the boulevard, the modernist cinema, **Kino International**
(No. 33), designed by the same architect (Josef Kaiser), is no less
impressive in its embodiment of the Soviet modernist style.

Karl-Marx-Allee • U-Bahn: Strausberger Platz

East Side Gallery

6 Stretching 0.8 mile (1.3 km) along Mühlenstrasse on the east bank of the Spree River, the East Side Gallery is the longest remaining section of the Berlin Wall. It features more than 100 paintings by artists from all over the world, most of whom came to daub their satirical comments onto the bare concrete slabs of the wall when the gallery opened in 1990. Highlights include German artist Birgit Kinder's painting of a Trabant breaking through the wall (pictured p. 125) and Russian artist Dmitri Vrubel's portrait of communist leaders Honecker and Brezhnev sharing their legendary brotherly kiss (pictured below). Beyond the wall you'll see the redbrick towers of **Oberbaumbrücke.** This bridge served as a Berlin Wall border crossing during the Cold War and, as such, marks a fitting end to this tour of Berlin's east.

Mühlenstrasse • www.eastsidegallery-berlin.de • U-Bahn: Warschauer Strasse

Dmitri Vrubel's painting bears the caption: "My God, help me to survive this deadly love."

Gedenkstätte Berliner Mauer

*A stretch of the former Berlin Wall now serves as
a dedicated Berlin Wall Memorial.*

The Window of Remembrance shows the faces of those who fell trying to escape.

This memorial to the Berlin Wall stretches the entire 0.75-mile length (1.2 km)
of Bernauer Strasse and is by far the best site from which to appreciate the
physical and psychological effects of one of the most brutal divisions of the
20th century. The East–West border dissected Bernauer Strasse in two,
separating neighbors on one side of the street from those on the other. Today,
steel poles have replaced the wall, marking out its original path. They lead you
north, from one exhibit to the next, starting at the Visitor Center.

■ VISITOR CENTER

Start at the Visitor Center for an overview of the site and its various exhibits. As you exit, don't miss the large photograph on the side of the building opposite, depicting this section of the border strip in 1989.

■ WINDOW OF REMEMBRANCE

This series of windows commemorates the 136 people who lost their lives due to the wall. Its goal—to individualize the victims with photos, names, and birth and death dates—is reinforced by the ever present array of personally placed flowers, stones, and candles.

■ DEATH STRIP

Drop into the **Documentation Center** for an exhibition on the street's history. Climb to the top of the adjacent **viewing platform** for a physical (and sobering) overview of the site. You'll be looking down, specifically, onto a 230-foot-long section (70 m) of Death Strip, complete with Stasi watchtower.

■ CHAPEL OF RECONCILIATION

This distinctively round, wooden-slatted chapel was built as a memorial to the original church on this

site, which was dramatically and controversially demolished by the East German government in 1985 to make way for border expansions. At noon on Tuesday through Friday, a prayer service commemorates a different victim of the Berlin Wall.

■ BORDER HOUSE

A little farther on from the chapel, the exposed remains of a former border house are accompanied by an exhibit on the lives of the residents and some of the escape attempts made. A marked trail highlights **Tunnel 57**— one of the most audacious of the Berlin Wall escapes, in which a 39-foot-long tunnel (12 m) allowed some 57 people to escape in 1964.

Bernauer Strasse • www.berliner-mauer-gedenkstaette.de • 030 46 79 86 66 6 • Visitor Center closed Mon. • S-Bahn: Nordbahnhof

The Trendy East

Following the collapse of the Berlin Wall, the vast migration from east to west was accompanied by a steady trickle in the other direction as artists and property developers vied for buildings in the city's eastern districts. For a quarter of a century the two groups have waged a battle of the creative over the commercial, of the squat over the penthouse, and it is not over yet.

In its heyday, almost every surface of Kunsthaus Tacheles was painted—inside and out. Opposite: The huge gallery space at Hamburger Bahnhof

The migrants set their sights on areas in Mitte, Prenzlauer Berg, and Friedrichshain, whose proximity to the Berlin Wall—both to the east and to the west—had made them, if not uninhabitable, certainly undesirable. The abundance of cheap and derelict housing in these areas was fertile ground for creative and commercial types. While artists, poets, and punks set up squats, underground nightclubs, and impromptu art galleries in abandoned industrial buildings, property developers embarked on a rigorous program of gentrification.

Battle of the Giants

Today, Berlin's subculture of graffiti and techno-clubbing is legendary. It draws big artists and even bigger crowds and is a major contributor to the city's economy. But the property developers want more of the action. In 2013, **Kunsthaus Tacheles,** a landmark squat in Mitte, was closed down and earmarked for redevelopment. Renowned for its ad hoc bars, alternative vibe, and graffiti-scrawled walls, the building had been at the epicenter of Berlin's hip art scene since the 1990s, when a group of artists rescued it from demolition. Its closure exposed the inevitable demise of the alternative scene that comes with the spread of commercialism, and the battle looks set to continue as more squats and nightclubs come under threat. In the meantime, the east remains a hub of art, design, and fashion—it's just that most of the action is happening in shiny new buildings instead of graffiti-covered squats.

Art Action

With an edgy mix of underground bars and independent galleries, the part of Mitte formerly known as Spandauer Vorstadt—the streets south of (and including) Torstrasse that flow between Alte Schönhauser Strasse and Oranienburger Strasse—remains Berlin's primary art hub. **Auguststrasse**

MUST-SEE **GALLERIES**

The Sammlung Boros
Berlin's most unique modern art venue is set in a World War II bunker. **Reinhardtstrasse 20, www.sammlung-boros.de, 030 27 59 40 65, €€€, closed Mon.–Wed.**

Hamburger Bahnhof A collection of contemporary art, plus regular exhibitions from international artists. **Invalidenstrasse 50–51, www .hamburgerbahnhof.de, 030 39 78 34 11, €€€, closed Mon.**

Sammlung Hoffmann
An impeccable collection of 20th-century art. **Sophie-Gips-Höfe, Sophienstrasse 21, www.sammlung-hoffmann .de, 030 28 49 91 20, €€, closed Aug.**

is recognized as Berlin's unofficial art mile—so-called for the sheer number of art galleries that line the street. The **Kunst-Werke Gallery** (*Auguststrasse 69, 030 24 34 59, €, closed Tues.*) is a dedicated space for uncompromising, cutting-edge art. Next door, **me Collectors Room** (*Auguststrasse 68, www.me-berlin.com, 030 86 00 85 10, €€, closed Mon.*) juxtaposes modern and ancient art and artifacts and includes a wonderful Cabinet of Curiosities.

Fashion Parade

Fashion is a big deal in Berlin, with **Bread & Butter** (*Münzstrasse 13, www.breadandbutter.com, 030 40 04 40*) organizing the city's biggest annual fashion trade show. The city's eastern districts have nurtured an army of local designers that includes **Claudia Skoda** (*Mulackstrasse 8, www.claudiaskoda.com, 030 40 04 18 84, closed Sun.*). Having started out in the 1970s, Skoda designs exclusive knitwear that remains as au courant around the world as it ever was. More recent appearances on the fashion scene include Alexandra Fischer-Roehler and Johanna

A Bread & Butter concept store

Kühl *(Linienstrasse 44, www.kaviargauche.com, 030 28 87 35 62),* whose elegant, feminine, and street-savvy **Kaviar Gauche** label launched in 2005.

Boutiques that line Alte Schönhauser Strasse and the surrounding streets of Spandauer Vorstadt include **Schwarzhogerzeil** *(Mulackstrasse 28, www .schwarzhogerzeil.de, 030 28 87 38 68),* specializing in top-end clothing and jewelry.

Club Scene

A major hub for squatters and anarchists during the 1990s, the Friedrichshain neighborhood has all but succumbed to the gentrification trend in recent years. Much of the action is centered on and around Boxhagener Platz, whose surrounding streets are awash with galleries, shops, cafés, and bars.

It is also here that clubbers will find the heavyweights of Berlin's nightclub scene. Legendary techno-haunt **Berghain** *(Am Wriezener Bahnhof, www.berghain.de, 030 29 00 05 97, €€€, closed Mon.–Thurs.)* lies on the border with Kreuzberg. The sprawling **RAW-tempel Gelände** *(Revaler Strasse 99, 030 29 24 69 5),* a sustainable urban project created from a former railway depot, also hosts a cluster of clubs. Among these you'll find the techno-electro **Suicide Circus** *(www.suicide-berlin .com, €€, closed Mon.–Tues.)* and **Cassiopeia** *(www.cassiopeia-berlin.de, 030 47 38 59 49, closed Mon.–Tues.),* where an eclectic playlist includes everything from grunge and electro, to hip-hop and reggae. With its 1950s' former-GDR (DDR) interior, and room for 1,500 guests, **Astra Kulturhaus** *(030 20 05 67 67),* within the same complex, regularly hosts spectacular live music events.

**Clubbing at Berghain
in Friedrichshain**

Beer Gardens

From spring to late September, Berliners look to the city's laid-back beer gardens to while away an afternoon or evening. Quench your thirst and soak up a little Berlin spirit in one of these leafy retreats. You'll find a good range of beverages beyond beer—as well as traditional rustic snacks.

■ PRATER

The Prater complex in Prenzlauer Berg is a Berlin institution dating back to the mid-19th century. There's nothing fancy here—just simple wooden benches and tables shaded by chestnut trees. Self-service kiosks sell a range of snacks, including sausages, soup, pretzels, and salad. Drink like a local and try the Prater Pils. If you want to out yourself as a tourist, ask for a Berliner Weisse, which comes with a shot of green or red syrup.

Kastanienallee 7–9 • www.pratergarten.de • 030 44 85 68 8 • € • Closed Oct.–March • U-Bahn: Eberswalder Strasse

■ CAFÉ AM NEUEN SEE

Perhaps Berlin's closest take on the Bavarian beer garden, this lakeside venue in the Tiergarten district draws large crowds in summer. Bavarian pretzels and *Leberkäse* (a traditional Bavarian meat loaf) are standard fare, but you can order pizza, too. Arrive early to grab a shady spot. This is a family friendly establishment, with a sandbox for children.

Lichtensteinallee 2 • 030 25 44 93 0 • €€ • S-Bahn/U-Bahn: Zoologischer Garten

■ SCHLEUSENKRUG

This Tiergarten favorite overlooks a stretch of Berlin's Landwehrkanal— the canal that runs from Friedrichshain in the east, through Kreuzberg, and on to Tiergarten in the west. Try one of their draft beers, then sit back and watch as canal boats negotiate the lock.

Müller-Breslau-Strasse • www.schleusenkrug.de • 030 31 39 90 9 • €€ • S-Bahn/U-Bahn: Zoologischer Garten

■ GOLGATHA

Head to Kreuzberg's Viktoriapark, where Golgatha caters to all tastes.

Visitors to the Tiergarten district take time out at the Schleusenkrug beer garden.

Less firmly focused on beer than the Prater, the Golgatha is good for breakfasts, coffee, cake in the afternoon, and predinner cocktails. The grill gets going at midday, and the restaurant serves soups and salads, too. There's dancing here on Friday and Saturday evenings.

Via Viktoriapark or Katzbachstrasse • www .golgatha-berlin.de • 030 78 52 45 3 • € • Closed Oct.–March • S-Bahn/U-Bahn: Yorckstrasse

■ Brauhaus Südstern
Here's a welcome twist: a beer garden with its own brewery. This Kreuzberg spot on the edge of Volkspark Hasenheide is a quiet place to chill. The home-brewed beers are complemented by hearty fare.

Hasenheide 69 • www.brauhaus-suedstern.de • 030 69 00 16 24 • € • U-Bahn: Südstern

■ Luise
A short walk from the **Botanischer Garten** (see p. 161) in Dahlem, this laid-back, family-friendly beer garden serves classic German dishes from an outdoor grill.

Königin-Luise-Strasse 40–42 • 030 84 18 88 0 • € • U-Bahn: Dahlem-Dorf

Schöneberg & Kreuzberg

Each of the districts that make up Berlin's western inner-city neighborhood has its own distinct character. From west to east, the tranquil charm of Schöneberg's beautifully landscaped squares gives way to the laid-back, anything-goes atmosphere of West Kreuzberg, which then explodes into the vibrant and colorful street-life of East Kreuzberg. These characteristics owe much to the area's past. Schöneberg was a hub for left-wing intellectuals during the Weimar years, while many of the Turkish *Gastarbeiters* (guest-workers) who helped rebuild and stimulate the city's postwar economy settled in Kreuzberg. Now that inner-city rents have risen, an influx of artists seeking more affordable lifestyles have added a new, bohemian vibe to the neighborhood.

◀ **Kreuzberg is renowned for its brightly painted facades. The words on the balcony offer a Turkish "welcome."**

Schöneberg & Kreuzberg

This tour carves a cultural path through the city and explores the ambience of each distinct area as well as the neighborhood's key sights.

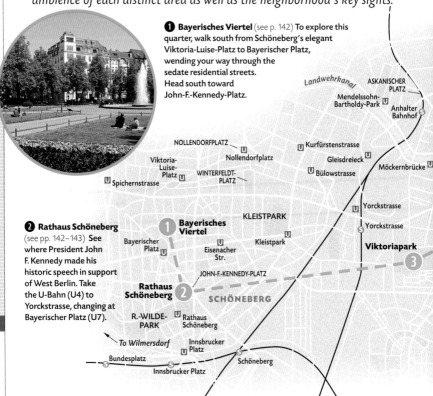

❶ Bayerisches Viertel (see p. 142) **To explore this quarter, walk south from Schöneberg's elegant Viktoria-Luise-Platz to Bayerischer Platz, wending your way through the sedate residential streets. Head south toward John-F.-Kennedy-Platz.**

❷ Rathaus Schöneberg (see pp. 142–143) **See where President John F. Kennedy made his historic speech in support of West Berlin. Take the U-Bahn (U4) to Yorckstrasse, changing at Bayerischer Platz (U7).**

❸ Viktoriapark (see pp. 143–144) Admire this park's tumbling waterfall and far-reaching views before leaving from its northern side. Walk east toward Bergmannstrasse and into Kreuzberg.

❹ West Kreuzberg (see p. 144) Explore the numerous boutique stores, cafés, and restaurants on and around Bergmannstrasse, then cross the Landwehrkanal at Lindenstrasse.

Map labels: Landwehrkanal · ASKANISCHER PLATZ · Mendelssohn-Bartholdy-Park · Anhalter Bahnhof · NOLLENDORFPLATZ · Kurfürstenstrasse · Nollendorfplatz · Gleisdreieck · Möckernbrücke · Viktoria-Luise-Platz · WINTERFELDT-PLATZ · Bülowstrasse · Spichernstrasse · Yorckstrasse · Yorckstrasse · KLEISTPARK · Bayerisches Viertel · Bayerischer Platz · Eisenacher Str. · Kleistpark · Viktoriapark · JOHN-F-KENNEDY-PLATZ · Rathaus Schöneberg · SCHÖNEBERG · R.-WILDE-PARK · Rathaus Schöneberg · To Wilmersdorf · Innsbrucker Platz · Bundesplatz · Innsbrucker Platz · Schöneberg

**SCHÖNEBERG & KREUZBERG DISTANCE: 6.5 MILES (10.5 KM)
TIME: APPROX. 8 HOURS U-BAHN START: VIKTORIA-LUISE-PLATZ**

⑤ Jüdisches Museum (see pp. 148–149) Daniel Libeskind's zinc-clad building is a fitting setting for the Jewish Museum. Continue a short way north on Lindenstrasse, turning right and then left onto Alte Jakobstrasse.

⑥ Berlinische Galerie (see p. 145) Take a short break in the gallery's convivial café, before viewing works by the city's most significant artists from 1870 to the present. Continue north on Alter Jakobstrasse to Oranienstrasse, then east to Kottbusser Tor.

⑧ Kreuzkölln (see pp. 146–147) Stroll along the Landwehrkanal on Maybachufer and head south to explore trendy Kreuzkölln, before winding up in one of its hip bars for well-deserved refreshment.

⑦ Kottbusser Tor (see p. 146) The area around Kottbusser Tor is electric day and night. Soak up the atmosphere and enjoy some Turkish or Middle Eastern food, then return to the canal on Kottbusser Damm.

Albert Einstein lived in the Bayerisches Viertel from 1918 to 1933.

Bayerisches Viertel

1 **Viktoria-Luise-Platz** lies at the center of Schöneberg's elegant Bavarian Quarter. Developed during the late 19th century, the area became a cultural hub during the Weimar era (see pp. 64–65). Today, the square retains the geometric landscaping of its original design. A number of pathways radiate from a central fountain, and there are colonnades beneath which you can sit and admire the immaculate topiary.

Film director Billy Wilder lived here *(No. 11)* as a young scriptwriter and Albert Einstein lived nearby *(Haberlandstrasse 8)*. Farther south, **Bayerischer Platz** was once home to psychoanalyst-philosopher Erich Fromm *(No. 1)*.

Walking the streets of this neighborhood, you'll notice colorful images on signs attached to lampposts—a loaf of bread here, a walking stick there. Read the text on the reverse to find simplified versions of anti-Semitic laws introduced by the Nazis in the 1930s: "Berlin Jews may only buy provisions from 4–5 p.m." and "Jewish doctors may no longer practice." Known as **Orte des Erinnerns** (Places of Remembrance), the signs—80 of them in total—urge us to reflect on the persecution of Berlin's Jews, some 16,000 of whom lived in this area before the Holocaust.

Between Viktoria-Luise-Platz and Bayerischer Platz • U-Bahn: Viktoria-Luise-Platz

Rathaus Schöneberg

2 Schöneberg Town Hall was the seat of West Berlin's government from 1948 to 1990. It stands in John-F.-Kennedy-Platz, so named following the 35th U.S. president's assassination. It was here that John F. Kennedy delivered his *"Ich bin ein Berliner"* ("I am a Berliner") speech on June 26, 1963, indicating U.S. support for West Berlin following the erection of the Berlin Wall.

Inside the building, aside from the grand staircases and walkways—mostly reconstructed—you can admire historical paintings, a bust of Friedrich Ebert, Germany's first president, and views from the **clock tower** *(guided tours only),* where a copy of the **Liberty Bell** chimes the time. The United States presented the bell to Berlin in 1950. There is also a permanent exhibition here about Jewish life in the neighborhood. Entitled **"We were neighbors once—biographies of Jewish contemporary witnesses,"** the exhibition relates the lives of 131 local Jews from the turn of the 20th century to the aftermath of World War II.

Whatever day of the week you visit Schöneberg Town Hall, you'll likely find a market in full swing in John-F.-Kennedy-Platz. On weekdays the stalls sell food, while on weekends, it's a popular flea market that attracts locals to the square (see p. 152).

John-F.-Kennedy-Platz • 030 90 27 70 • U-Bahn: Rathaus Schöneberg

Viktoriapark

3 West Kreuzberg's Viktoriapark is crowned by Friedrich Schinkel's majestic monument commemorating Prussian victory in the War of Liberation against Napoleon. From the monument, an impressive man-made waterfall tumbles 80 feet (24 m) down to street level (summertime only). A couple of small vineyards—one of which produces around 200 bottles of wine per year—

The waterfall at Viktoriapark and the monument that gave Kreuzberg its name

cover the park's southern slopes, and you'll find the seasonal beer garden **Golgatha** (*closed Oct.–March*; see pp. 136–137) in the southwest corner. If you are visiting Berlin in late summer, you'll catch the annual **Kreuzberger Festliche Tage,** a Festive Days Funfair (*last week Aug./first week Sept.*), with a diverse two-week program of events for all.

Viktoriapark • U-Bahn: Yorckstrasse

GOOD **EATS**

■ RENGER PATZSCH

A sophisticated wood-paneled dining room, a changing daily menu that includes some new takes on German classics, and great service make this one of Schöneberg's finest dining experiences. **Wartburgstrasse 54, 030 78 42 0 59, €€**

■ SAUVAGE

Dairy foods, refined sugar, gluten, grains, and vegetable oils are off-limits in this Paleo restaurant that specializes in organic meat, fish, and veg. **Pflügerstrasse 25, 030 53 16 75 47, €€**

■ UFERPAVILLON

This low-key kiosk with canalside tables and chairs runs a simple menu with dishes that change daily—schnitzel and French fries or herb-crusted fish with rice—as well as crisp, hot waffles. **Uferpromenade at Paul-Lincke-Ufer 030 74 00 69 81, €**

West Kreuzberg

④ West Kreuzberg, referred to by locals as 61 after its pre-reunification zip code, is more relaxed than its eastern counterpart, SO36 (see p. 146). Lined with lively restaurants, cafés, and trendy boutiques, Bergmannstrasse and its surrounding streets epitomize this laid-back part of the city. Simply stroll through the area and you'll soon succumb to its relaxed ambience. Step into the **Markthalle am Marheinekeplatz** (*Marheinekeplatz 15, www.meine-markthalle.de, 030 61 28 61 46, closed Sun.*) for fresh, high-quality, local foods and produce from all over the world. With a restaurant, cafés, and all manner of food stands, this is an ideal spot to stop for lunch or a snack. Alternatively, head to **Barcomi's Café** (*Bergmannstrasse 21*), sister venue to the top brunch spot in the Scheunenviertel (see p. 68) and a favorite with locals.

Bergmannstrasse and around • U-Bahn: Gneisenaustrasse

Jüdisches Museum

⑤ See pp. 148–149.

Lindenstrasse 9–14 • www.jmberlin.de • 030 25 99 33 00 • €€ • Closed Rosh Hashanah, Yom Kippur, and Dec. 24 • U-Bahn: Kochstrasse

SCHÖNEBERG & KREUZBERG

Two stairways crisscross at the center of the lofty main hall at the Berlinische Galerie.

Berlinische Galerie

6 This modern, spacious whitewashed gallery in a former glass warehouse showcases Berlin-made modern art, photography, and architecture. The ground floor is dedicated to temporary exhibitions while, upstairs, a permanent exhibition spans the major German art movements between 1870 and the present day with works by Max Liebermann, Felix Nussbaum, Otto Dix, and George Grosz always on display. Among the more quirky exhibits is **Pulvarium** (2005) by Jenny Michel and Michael Hoepfel, a vast collection of dust bunnies, pinned and mounted like butterflies in 40 specimen cases, each one labeled using a system not unlike Carl Linnaeus's binomial nomenclature. The stylish **Café Dix,** with its purple-and-white interior and sun terrace, is a great place to peruse the program of upcoming exhibitions, screenings, and art classes.

Alte Jakobstrasse 124–128 • www.berlinischegalerie.de • 030 78 90 26 00 • €€ (free first Mon. of the month) • Closed Tues., Dec. 24 and 31 • U-Bahn: Kochstrasse

Kottbusser Tor

7 Lively East Kreuzberg, also known as SO36, is grittier than **West Kreuzberg** (see p. 144) and has more of an inner-city buzz. Its hub, Kottbusser Tor, has earned the moniker **Little Istanbul** owing to the high number of Turkish inhabitants renting apartments in the 1950s' housing projects that flank the area. Visit on a Tuesday or Friday afternoon and jostle with locals at the Turkish market (see p. 152) that lines **Maybachufer**— the south bank of the Landwehrkanal.

An early electric kettle designed by Peter Behrens for AEG, on show at the Museum der Dinge

North of Kottbusser Tor, independent stores, cafés, and bars line Oranienstrasse, including the legendary **SO36** (*Oranienstrasse 190, 030 61 40 13 06*), a bastion of punk rock and other new wave music since the 1970s. Farther along, the engaging **Museum der Dinge** (Museum of Things; *Oranienstrasse 25, www.museumderdinge.de, 030 92 10 63 11, €€, closed Tues.–Wed., and May 1*) traces a history of German design via cabinets of curiosities, from pots and pans to key chains. In summer Moritzplatz hosts the **Prinzessinnengarten** (*Prinzessinnenstrasse 35–38, www.prinzessinnengarten.net, closed Nov.–mid-May*), a community gardening project, where you can relax in the garden café.

Intersection of Skalitzer Strasse and Kottbusser Damm • U-Bahn: Kottbusser Tor

Kreuzkölln

8 Berliners have dubbed the area immediately south of the Landwehrkanal, Kreuzkölln. The name is a mash-up of Kreuzberg to the west and Neukölln to the south. This district exudes a homegrown atmosphere of boho gentrification, thanks to its multitude of fashion boutiques, art spaces, cocktail bars, and interesting combinations of all three, such as **Sing Blackbird** (*Sanderstrasse 11, 030 54 84 50 51*), where you can buy vintage clothing from the 1970s to the 1990s, eat vegan food on mismatched china in its adjoining café, and sometimes catch an exhibition or a movie.

Farther south is **Weserstrasse**, one of the trendier streets that runs into the Neukölln district, a once gritty working-class neighborhood that is now on the cusp of gentrification. Here Turkish döner shops vie with classy wine bars, including **Vin Aqua Vin** (*Weserstrasse 204, 030 94 05 28 86*), and café-bars such as **Ä** (*Weserstrasse 40, 030 17 74 06 38 37*), whose grungy interior draws a cool-but-casual clientele for concerts, storytelling evenings, and more.

East of Kottbusser Damm • U-Bahn: Schönleinstrasse

SCHÖNEBERG & KREUZBERG

Neukölln's Ä bar epitomizes the cool, urban atmosphere of this trendy neighborhood.

Jüdisches Museum

Berlin's Jewish Museum records the horrors of the Holocaust and explores the history of Jewish-German relations before and since.

Libeskind's brutal exterior of the Jewish Museum presents a challenge from the offset.

Designed by renowned American architect Daniel Libeskind, Berlin's Jewish Museum, a defiantly angular building clad in zinc, with violent gashes for windows, forms a dislocated Star of David when seen from above. From the 18th-century Collegienhaus (Old Building), a venue for concerts and events, a black slate gangway leads to the museum's Trio of Axes—three deliberately askew and overlapping corridors that take you on a 2,000-year journey through the history of Jewish people in Germany.

From the Old Building, descend to the museum's Trio of Axes, all of which start in the same place. Below is the recommended order for seeing them.

■ AXIS OF THE HOLOCAUST

Eerily lit display cases contain the poignant possessions of those who died in the Holocaust and accounts of those who escaped it. They include the personal mementos of Leo Scheuer, who eluded the Nazis by hiding in a hole in the ground for 15 months, and the letters of "Aimee and Jaguar"—a lesbian Jewish-German couple who were separated by the Nazis.

■ VOIDED VOID

At the end of the Axis of the Holocaust stands the **Holocaust Tower,** a silo with a tiny slit at the top to admit light and sound. There is a metal ladder on one wall, but it is out of reach. Cold and dark, the space creates a deeply unsettling representation of captivity. Libeskind calls this space a voided void. It is one of several empty spaces that extend to the building's full height, glimpsed now and then through slits in the museum walls. Barred to the public, the voids represent the absence of Jews.

SAVVY **TRAVELER**

When you buy a ticket to either the Jüdisches Museum or the Berlinische Galerie, you will receive a reduction on a ticket for the other, either on the day of the visit or for the following two days. On Monday, the museum stays open until 9 p.m., and the restaurant, which specializes in new twists on traditional Jewish food, remains open until 10 p.m.

■ AXIS OF EXILE

This uneven and gradually narrowing walkway leads outside the main building to the **Garden of Exile**—49 concrete columns erected on a slanting floor. The exhibit represents the alien and unnerving experience of exile.

■ AXIS OF CONTINUITY

This, the longest of the three corridors, winds through the main exhibition on Jewish-German relations through the centuries. Spread over two floors, artifacts span personal histories and public developments. Paintings of Jewish luminaries such as Albert Einstein hang beside drawings of the ghetto and posters advertising Jewish goods and services. Interactive media help set the items in context.

SCHÖNEBERG & KREUZBERG

Lindenstrasse 9–14 • www.jmberlin.de • 030 25 99 33 00 • €€ • Closed Rosh Hashanah, Yom Kippur, and Dec. 24 • U-Bahn: Kochstrasse

City of Diversity

Around half a million Berlin residents—more than 10 percent of the city's population—are of foreign nationality, while another 100,000 naturalized Berliners have a migrant background. Walk the streets of central Berlin and German is the lingua franca. Head a little south or east of the center, however, and Turkish or Vietnamese voices are more likely to meet your ears.

Ghanaian dancers take to the streets in the Karneval der Kulturen festival.
Opposite: Locals sample the Turkish delights at the twice-weekly market on Maybachufer in Kreuzberg.

SCHÖNEBERG & KREUZBERG

Guest-workers

Postwar immigration began in West Germany during the 1950s. The government recruited immigrants in as *Gastarbeiter* (guest-workers), not only to compensate for the country's postwar labor shortage, but also to assist with the so-called *Wirtschaftswunder* (Economic Miracle) of the 1960s and 1970s. It was of benefit to the West's Cold War strategy that Germany—being on the East–West border—was seen to be booming, thanks to U.S. Marshall Plan subsidies aimed at rebuilding Europe.

The largest group of immigrants were Turks, who began arriving in October 1961. Initially, the government limited the length of time guest-workers could stay in Germany to one year. Other restrictions—relating to housing, education, and family reunion—also applied. Decades passed before workers eventually became permanent residents, settling in Berlin with their families.

Although the Turkish community remains the largest ethnic group in Berlin, a second wave of immigrants swept in from Eastern Europe in the 1980s. Known as *Aussiedler* (resettlers), they comprised ethnic Germans from Romania, Poland, and the collapsing states of the former Soviet Union.

Cultural Legacy

Around 200 different countries are represented in Berlin today—a hodgepodge of non-German communities living side by side in the traditional immigrant districts of Kreuzberg, Tiergarten, Neukölln, and Schöneberg. The streets may be western European architecturally, but many of the storefronts tell a different story, packed as they are with colorful clothing and ethnic foodstuffs. For four days in May, the Karneval der Kulturen (Carnival of Cultures; *www.karneval-berlin.de*) celebrates the city's diversity with events centered around a parade through the streets of Kreuzberg.

ETHNIC **EATERIES**

Cô Cô This tiny Vietnamese restaurant in the Mitte district is popular for its meat- or vegetable-filled baguettes (*banh mi*) **Rosenthaler Strasse 2, 030 24 63 05 95, €**

Defne Dine on Turkish classics while overlooking the Landwehrkanal. **Planufer 92c, 030 81 79 71 11, €€**

Maly Ksiaze Polish sweet and savory dumplings (*pierogi*) in the heart of Kreuzberg. **Lillienthalstrasse 6, 030 62 90 80 68, €**

Maroush Traditional Lebanese fare at very reasonable prices. **Adalbertstrasse 93, 030 69 53 61 71, €**

Street Markets

Almost every neighborhood in Berlin has its own street market selling produce, secondhand furniture, street food, and often all three. Those in the inner-city areas pull in the biggest crowds, and the food stalls on Winterfeldtplatz and Mauerpark's flea market draw foodies and vintage fans from all over town.

■ SCHÖNEBERG

Operating every Saturday since 1990, this weekly market on **Winterfeldtplatz** (*www.winterfeldt-markt.de, 8 a.m.–4 p.m.*) has mushroomed from a couple of stalls to more than 200 today, selling meat, fish, produce, clothes, and flowers. It is now open on Wednesday mornings (*8 a.m.–2 p.m.*) as well. Meanwhile, a daily food market sets up on **John-F.-Kennedy-Platz** during the week (see p. 142). The square also hosts a weekend flea market (*both 8 a.m.–4 p.m., flea market Sat.–Sun.*).

■ KREUZBERG

For an authentic Turkish bazaar vibe, head to the busy market on Landwehrkanal's **Maybachufer** on Tuesday or Friday (*11 a.m.–6:30 p.m.*). **Markthalle 9** (*Eisenbahnstrasse 42/43, www.markthalleneun.de*) hosts a farmers market on Fridays and Saturdays (*10 a.m.–6 p.m.*), street food on Thursday evenings (*5 p.m.–10 p.m.*), and food events at other times.

■ MITTE

On weekends, Central Mitte holds an arts market between Schlossbrücke and Museumsinsel (*10 a.m.–4 p.m.*) selling books, photographs, and paintings. There is a weekend flea market (*Sat.–Sun., 11 a.m.–5 p.m.*) with around 60 stalls near the Bode-Museum (see sidebar p. 75) farther along the river. A twice-weekly market at **Hackescher Markt** (*Thurs., 9 a.m.–6 p.m., Sat. 10 a.m.–6 p.m.*) sells food, leather goods, jewelry, watches, and arts and crafts.

■ CHARLOTTENBURG

One of the biggest and most famous weekend flea markets in Berlin spreads over sprawling Strasse des 17. Juni (*Sat.–Sun., 10 a.m.–5 p.m.*). Here,

SCHÖNEBERG & KREUZBERG

A lively flea market sprawls over the cobblestones in the Mauerpark on Sundays.

you'll find secondhand antiques, vinyl, and an arts market—prices aren't cheap and bargains are rare, but the atmosphere is great.

■ PRENZLAUER BERG

A Saturday farmers market on pretty **Kollwitzplatz** *(9 a.m.–5 p.m.)* sells high-end produce from nearby farms—perfect for summer picnics. A smaller version of the market takes place every Thursday *(9 a.m.–4 p.m.)*. On Sundays, Berliners flock to the flea market at **Mauerpark** *(Bernauer Strasse 63–64, www.mauerparkmarkt .de, 8 a.m.–6 p.m.)* for clothes, records,

and antiques. On Sundays, retro design pieces and vintage furniture, clothes, and shoes are the draw at **Arkonaplatz** *(10 a.m.–4 p.m.)*.

■ FRIEDRICHSHAIN

An upbeat crowd throngs to the Saturday food market on **Boxhagener Platz** *(9 a.m.–3:30 p.m.)*. Some come specifically for the freshly cooked street food, such as Turkish *gözleme* (savory pastries), grilled fish, and bruschetta. On Sundays, a flea market *(10 a.m.–8 p.m.)* sells the usual assemblage of vinyl, jewelry, books, and vintage curiosities.

Dahlem & the West

Berlin's leafy western suburbs delight and surprise visitors, especially in summer. Just past the borders of Charlottenburg stands the Olympiastadion, the first large-scale architectural project undertaken by the Nazis and a striking symbol of their oppressive power. From the stadium, the vast Grunewald forest stretches south, crossed by walking and cycling trails and lapped by the Grunewaldsee. On the shore of the lake, Jagdschloss Grunewald, a 16th-century hunting lodge, displays paintings by masters of the German Renaissance. Just to the west of here are the watery attractions of the Havel River and the popular Wannsee area with its island and beaches, while to the east, sleepy Dahlem offers excellent museums, Saturday markets, and world-class botanical gardens.

◀ **Yachts and kayaks
glide through the
water with idyllic
views across the
Grunewaldsee.**

Dahlem & the West

Reminders of Berlin's checkered past combine with a world-class museum and botanical gardens on this walk on the west side.

5 Museen Dahlem (see pp. 162–163)
Complete your tour browsing several thousand years of pan-cultural history at this purpose-built museum complex.

4 Botanischer Garten
(see p. 161) Explore Berlin's botanical gardens, with landscaped Italian gardens, 19th-century greenhouses, and an arboretum. Retrace your steps on Königin-Luise-Strasse.

1 Olympiastadion (see pp. 158–159)
Built by the Nazis for the 1936 Olympics, this stadium is now used for sports events and concerts. Stroll the grounds or join a tour. Take the U-Bahn to Oskar-Helene-Heim, then walk 1 mile (2 km) north.

2 Jagdschloss Grunewald
(see p. 159) Now an art gallery, this 16th-century lakeside palace contains German and Dutch paintings and hunting-related paraphernalia. A 20-minute stroll through the forest will bring you to the AlliiertenMuseum.

Spandauer See · HASELHORST · Ziatdelle · Haselhorst · Paulsternstrasse · Spree · Altstadt Spandau · SPANDAU · Spandau · Stresow · Ruhleben · CHARLOTTENBURG · REICHS- · Olympiastadion · Olympiastadion · OLYMPISCHER PLATZ · Olympia-stadion · Neu-Westend · Olympia-stadion **1** Olympiastadion · Pichelsberg · Theodor-Heuss-Platz · Kaiserdamm · Havel · HEERSTRASSE · PICHELSDORFER STR. · Scharfe

❸ Alliierten Museum

(see pp. 160–161) The former library and cinema of the Allied Powers documents the Cold War era. Exhibits include a plane used in the Berlin Airlift and a segment of the Allied spy tunnel. On leaving head north on Clayallee, then east on Königin-Luise-Strasse, passing by Museen Dahlem.

DAHLEM & THE WEST DISTANCE: 7.75 MILES (12.5 KM)
TIME: APPROX. 6.5 HOURS U-BAHN START: OLYMPIASTADION

Map labels

WILMERSDORF

HALENSEE

MASUREN ALLEE

Westkreuz

Halensee

Messe Süd

Teufelsberg ▲ 115 m

Grunewald

KOENIGSALLEE

HAGENSTR.

GRUNEWALD

HÜTTEN

GRUNEWALD

HAVELCHAUSSEE

Havel

Grosser Wannsee

WANNSEE

Nikolassee

NIKOLASSEE

Wannsee

SCHLACHTENSEE

Schlachtensee

Krumme Lanke

PAUL-ERNST-PARK

DÜPPEL

Mexikoplatz

ZEHLENDORF

Zehlendorf

Krumme Lanke

ARGENTINISCHE STR.

TOM-

Onkel Toms Hütte

Oskar-Helene-Heim

CLAYALLEE

Sundgauer Strasse

Lichterfelde-West

Botanischer Garten

❹ Botanischer Garten

❺ Dahlem-Dorf

Museen Dahlem-Kunst und Kulturen der Welt

PACELLIALLEE

DAHLEM

Podbielskiallee

Breitenbachplatz

SCHMARGENDORF

Heidelberger Platz

Hohenzollerndamm

HOHENZOLLERNDAMM

PÜCKLER-STRASSE

Grunewaldsee

CLAYALLEE

WEG

ONKEL-

ALLEE

❸ Alliierten Museum

❷ Jagdschloss Grunewald

0   1 mile
0   2 kilometers

U.S. sprinter Jesse Owens (right) storms to the finish line at the Berlin Olympics in 1936.

Olympiastadion

The 75,000-capacity Olympic Stadium, home to local soccer heroes Hertha BSC since 1963, has successfully hosted two FIFA World Cup competitions as well as pop luminaries, including the Rolling Stones and Madonna. Designed by the Nazis for the 1936 Olympics, the neoclassical structure—which survived the war almost intact—was modeled on Rome's Colosseum. The Nazis saw the Olympics as a chance to display Aryan superiority, a strategy that was undermined when African–American sprinter Jesse Owens won four gold medals, including the 100-meter dash.

You can tour the stadium and its grounds (*from 9 a. m.*), and it's worth investing in the audioguide (*€3*), which gives an hour's worth of historical and architectural information about the venue. Creating an imposing first impression on the east side of the stadium, the vast **Olympischer Platz** leads to two original stone pillars strung with the Olympic rings. Inside, a paved walkway circles the stadium, punctuated with engraved stone columns, 1930s' statuary, and the Olympic Bell, complete with Nazi insignia. The bell originally sat inside the 250-foot-high (76 m) **Glockenturm** (bell tower). Climb the bell tower *(opening hours vary—check the website before visiting)*, for views over Berlin's western suburbs and Grunewald. The stadium's swimming pool is open to the public in summer, when the **Waldbühne** *(www.waldbuehne-berlin.de)*, an open-air stage in Olympiapark, also hosts concerts (see p. 170).

Olympischer Platz 3 • www.olympiastadion-berlin.de • 030 25 00 23 22 • €€ (audioguide €3) • U-Bahn: Olympiastadion

SAVVY **TRAVELER**

Check venue websites for seasonal opening times. In winter, Jagdschloss Grunewald is only open on weekends and the Botanischer Garten closes at 4 p.m. Be sure to start early at Olympiastadion in order to get the most from each site.

Jagdschloss Grunewald

2 Sitting beside the forest-fringed waters of the Grunewaldsee, this 16th-century hunting lodge is the oldest of the many palaces, residences, and parks built in Berlin by the Hohenzollern dynasty. You can access the lodge—now an art gallery—via a leafy forest path popular with joggers, strollers, and dog-walkers. The **Great Hall** displays hunt-related artifacts: a tapestry from around 1700, hunting trophies and paintings, a double-barreled gun from 1550. Upstairs, Dutch and German paintings include nearly 30 by Lucas Cranach the Elder (1472–1553) and Younger (1515–1586). Stop for coffee and cake in the courtyard or take a stroll beside the lake.

Hüttenweg 100 • www.spsg.de • 030 81 33 59 7 • €€ • Closed Mon. year-round , and Tues.–Fri. Nov.–March • U-Bahn: Oskar-Helene-Heim

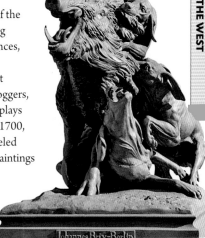

A statue of hunting dogs attacking a wild boar outside Jagdschloss Grunewald

AlliiertenMuseum

3 It is impossible to miss the Allied Museum, thanks to the **Hastings TG 503 aircraft** at the entrance. (From April through October, you can go inside the plane for a small fee.) The British plane was one of several hundred used to drop essential supplies into West Berlin during the Soviet blockade of the Allied sectors (see p. 165). At the peak of the airlift, one plane per minute touched down in Berlin.

The museum tells the story of the Western powers in Berlin during the postwar years until the reunification of the city in 1990. The two buildings on either side of the plane originally housed the **Outpost Theater** (cinema) and the Nicholson Memorial Library of the U.S. garrison. An exhibition in the former cinema focuses on the occupation of Berlin by the Allied troops, the airlift, and everyday life in the American, British, and French sectors. It includes a

The story of the Allied occupation of Berlin as told through exhibits at the AlliiertenMuseum

segment of the **spy tunnel** built by American and British intelligence services to tap the telephone lines of the Soviets. Exhibits in the former library focus on military confrontations between East and West during the Cold War. Outside the museum, you can climb aboard a railroad car from the French military train and enter the original guardhouse of **Checkpoint Charlie** (see p. 57).

Clayallee 135 • www.alliiertenmuseum.de • 030 81 81 99 0 • Closed Mon. • U-Bahn: Oskar-Helene-Heim

Botanischer Garten

4 Lose yourself for an hour or so in the verdant oases of Berlin's Botanical Garden—a whopping 106 acres (43 ha) with around 22,000 plant species. At the southern end, native woody plants and roses stock the arboretum, while to the north are the **Gewächshäuser**—an impressive group of glass and steel greenhouses. The largest has waterfalls and towering bamboo inside. Pick up a map at the entrance or, better still, one of four seasonal leaflets listing 12 blooms to discover on a dedicated trail.

The neighboring **Botanisches Museum** *(admission free with Botanical Garden ticket)* offers a chance to test and expand your knowledge via dioramas and magnified details of plant structures.

Königin-Luise-Strasse 6–8 • www.bgbm.org • 030 83 85 01 00 • €€ • U-Bahn: Dahlem-Dorf

Museen Dahlem

5 See pp. 162–163.

Lansstrasse 8/Arnimallee 23–27 • www.smb.museum • 030 26 64 24 24 2 • €€ • U-Bahn: Dahlem-Dorf

---

GOOD **EATS**

■ **CHALET SUISSE**
This restaurant in Grunewald serves French-Swiss dishes, including some game, in a relaxed, semirural setting. **Clayallee 99, 030 83 26 36 2, €€**

■ **DOMÄNE DAHLEM**
The farm shop in this 800-year-old working farm and open-air agrarian museum sells soups, cakes, sausages, and drinks, which can be eaten on one of the nearby picnic tables. **Königin-Luise-Strasse 49, 030 66 63 00 0, €**

■ **LUISE**
This elegant space serves draft beers, homemade burgers, and German specialties. There is also a beer garden, a children's playground, and an outdoor grill. **Königin-Luise-Strasse 40–42, 030 84 18 88 0, €**

DAHLEM & THE WEST

Museen Dahlem

Conveniently situated under one roof, this triad of museums presents history, art, and culture from around the world.

American stone figures and painted pottery at the Museum of Ethnology

The Museen Dahlem rank as Berlin's third most important cultural center after Museumsinsel (see pp. 74–75) and the Kulturforum (see p. 102). Housed in a turn-of-the-20th-century building, the center comprises the Museum of Ethnology, Museum of European Cultures, and Museum of Asian Art. Together they contain an impressive selection of exhibits from Berlin's global collections. Within the Museum of Ethnology, the JuniorMuseum hosts rotating exhibitions that introduce young children to non-European cultures.

With around half a million objects in the Museum of Ethnology alone, it would be impossible to see all three museums in their entirety. Take a detailed tour of just one museum or target highlights from each. Ticket price covers all three museums.

ETHNOLOGISCHES MUSEUM

The Museum of Ethnology displays objects from all corners of the Earth, accompanied by audio recordings, photographs, and film. On the ground floor, life-size boats from the South Pacific are the highlight of the **South Sea and Melanesia** collection. Also impressive are the outsized stone sculptures from the **Ancient American** collection, which include a massive stone stele from Guatemala.

On the upper floor, head straight for a full-scale traditional house and the displays of masks and ceremonial figures in the **Africa** collection.

MUSEUM FÜR ASIATISCHE KUNST

The Museum of Asian Art spans 4,000 years of Indo-Asian culture. Don't miss the iconic **"Teahouse"** by modern Chinese conceptual artist Ai Weiwei, composed of 378 cubes and 54 prisms of highly fragrant

compressed pu'er tea. Also of note are the ancient murals, paintings, and clay and wood sculptures from cave monasteries in Turfan, China, in the **East Asian Art** collection.

MUSEUM EUROPÄISCHER KULTUREN

Standouts at the collection of the Museum of European Cultures include a gleaming black gondola from Venice (1910) and the 40-foot-tall (12 m) **"Christmas Mountain"** from the Erzgebirge region of East Germany. Made up of more than 300 intricately crafted figures portraying the life of Christ, many of which move at the press of a button. This is a big hit with children, as are the European handicrafts markets held in the museum at Easter and other times (check the museum website for details of upcoming events during your stay).

DAHLEM & THE WEST

Lansstrasse 8/Arnimallee 23–27 • www.smb.museum • 030 26 64 24 24 2 • €€ • U-Bahn: Dahlem-Dorf

A Divided City

For four decades of the 20th century, Berlin symbolized a divided Europe. Split politically into East and West following World War II, the city was physically divided by a wall from 1961 until 1989. All but fragments of the Berlin Wall have gone now, but a legacy of division lives on among the city's inhabitants, some of whom look back with nostalgia to former times.

This emblem of a tank decorates a wall at the Soviet war memorial in Schönholzer Heide in former East Berlin. Opposite: A plane brings in much-needed supplies during the Berlin Airlift (1948–1949).

The End of World War II

When Germany capitulated to the Allies in May 1945, Soviet troops took control of Berlin. The victorious Allies met at Cecilienhof Palace in Potsdam in July to sketch out a new European order. They divided Germany into four zones (U.S., British, French, and Soviet). The capital, Berlin, was in the Soviet sector, but it, too, was split into four zones in what was to be a temporary military occupation.

One City: Four Zones

The Allies planned for a united Germany but could not come to a concrete arrangement with the Soviets. Frustrated by the lack of progress, the U.S., with some support from France and Britain, pressed ahead with economic reforms in West Berlin. In June 1948, the three Western Allies went a step farther by introducing a new currency for West Germany and West Berlin without consulting their Soviet partner.

By now it was clear that most Germans did not want to live under a communist system. Crucially, most felt great hostility toward their Soviet occupiers.

This was not just a legacy of Nazi propaganda. Soviet soldiers had raped, and sometimes murdered, thousands of women when they arrived in Berlin—in revenge for the similar atrocities committed by Nazi soldiers in the Soviet Union.

The Berlin Airlift

Moscow reacted with indignation to the currency reforms and imposed a blockade on overland routes connecting West Berlin with the Western Allies' occupied territory in western Germany. For 15 months from June 24, 1948 to May 12, 1949, West Berlin relied for its supplies on air convoys from the West to Tempelhof airport—a memorial to the event stands outside the terminal building. The story is also recounted (mainly from a U.S. perspective) at the **AlliiertenMuseum** (see pp. 160–161).

REMEMBERING
THE WALL

Several initiatives around Berlin recall life in the divided city. For an impressive and neutral narrative, head for the **Gedenkstätte Berliner Mauer** (see pp. 130–131). Stretching for almost a mile (2 km) along Bernauer Strasse, running northeast of Nordbahnhof, the memorial includes a stretch of the former wall, a museum, and a beautiful chapel. An exhibition at the **Tränenpalast** (*Reichstagufer 17, 30 46 77 77 90*) near Friedrichstrasse S-Bahn station recalls the leave-taking and tears that were once part of everyday life at this former crossing point between the two halves of Berlin.

The building of the wall left the 18th-century Brandenburg Gate marooned in East Germany, visible from the West but unreachable. When the wall came down in 1989 (opposite), the gate featured in many images of liberation.

Two German States

The Western Allies' decision in early 1949 to set up a separate country on their territory—the Federal Republic of Germany, known as West Germany, with a parliament in Bonn—further provoked the Soviet Union. West Berlin was never part of West Germany, but the enclave sent observers to the Bonn parliament. The Soviets, in turn, set up the German Democratic Republic in the east in October 1949.

The Building of the Wall

Arrangements for transit between East and West Berlin existed through the 1950s. Many Berliners lived in one half of the city but worked in the other. This made Berlin the focus of mass emigration from the east, with at least a quarter of the East German population voting with their feet.

In 1961, the East Germans built the Berlin Wall, severing almost all connections between the two halves of Berlin. It was understandable that the communist government wanted to stop the exodus, but as a symbol of their regime it was a propaganda catastrophe. Photographs of East Germans trying to flee across the barrier appeared in the Western media, contributing to the negative image of the communist regime, especially when those fleeing were shot dead.

The End of an Era

In the late 1980s, demonstrations in East German cities spurred the debate about change in the communist East. The Soviet Union took the lead in defusing Cold War tensions, and Mikhail Gorbachev's visit to Berlin on October 7, 1989, signaled this willingness to change. Ten days later veteran East German leader Erich Honecker resigned, and on November 9, 1989, the East German government announced the immediate opening of border crossings to the West. A year later, the two German states formally merged.

Legacy of the Wall

Few mourned the disappearance of the wall, but there are some in the east who regret losing the security and stability that came with a socialist society. In many ways, Berlin remains divided. The eastern half of the city still tends to vote for left-leaning political parties, and *solyanka* (a spicy soup) and other Russian dishes still feature on menus in the east. Some older West Berliners look back with affection to a time when Berlin was a western outpost behind the Iron Curtain. Berlin was quieter in those days—and hugely subsidized by the West. Yet it was not just a place for the privileged. Not having any military service, it was also a magnet for freethinkers and liberals. Their communes have almost disappeared as a unified Berlin asserts its status as a world city.

Summer in the City

In summer, Berlin really comes into its own. Cafés and bars spill out onto the sidewalks, and the buzz of endless parties and events, from street festivals to outdoor movies, fills the air. Rivers and lakes offer swimming and boating, and the city's parks provide plenty of spots to throw down a picnic blanket.

■ SWIMMING

Just west of Dahlem, and a world apart from Berlin's culture-swamped and often gritty inner-city, Wannsee is an idyllic summer playground. Its most obvious warm-weather attraction is the **Strandbad Wannsee** (Wannsee Beach; *Wannseebadweg, 030 78 73 25, €€, open mid-April– mid-Sept.*), one of Europe's largest and oldest outdoor lidos. An impressive sandy beach lined by rows of classic sausage, beer, and ice-cream stalls and dotted with wicker beach chairs stretches for more than a mile (1.6 km).

To swim in an outdoor pool head straight to **Sommerbad Kreuzberg** (*Prinzenstrasse 113–119, 030 61 61 08 0, €€, open June–mid-Sept.*), which has three swimming pools (one of which is unheated and chlorine-free), a large sunbathing area, and access to nearby Böcklerpark.

■ BEACH BARS

Even in the center of Berlin, you will find a surprising number of summer "beach bars"—places where you can feel sand beneath your feet, sit under a palm tree, and sometimes even swim or play volleyball. The season traditionally starts around Easter time and lasts as long as the sun keeps shining—often well into September. Recline in a deck chair, cocktail in hand, and watch the tourist boats go by at **Capital Beach Bar** (*Ludwig -Erhard-Ufer, 0163 56 54 12 2*), between the Reichstag and the Hauptbahnhof. Or head to **Strandbar Mitte** (*Monbijoupark, Oranienburger Strasse 78*), overlooking the Bode-Museum, where you can loll around in two-seater beach chairs (*Strandkörb*) or play volleyball.

If you're traveling with children, they'll love the children's beach in **Monbijoupark** (*Oranienburger Strasse,*

The lido at Strandbad Wannsee attracts thousands of visitors during summer.

030 33 39 50 9), close to the Neue Synagoge and Museumsinsel. There is lawn space for adults, an ice-cream kiosk, and a small playground.

■ SUMMER FESTIVALS

During Pentecost (late May/early June), Kreuzberg comes alive with the **Karneval der Kulturen** (*www.karneval-berlin.de*), a street festival celebrating the cultural diversity of Berlin with music, food, floats, and a grand parade. The carnival starts on Hermannplatz and continues to Möckernstrasse. It is an event that draws more than one million people.

North of the Tiergarten, the **Deutsch-Amerikanisches Volksfest** (German-American Peoples Festival; *Heidestrasse 30, www.deutsch-amerikanisches-volksfest.de, 030 16 34 00 05 00, end July–mid-Aug*) has been operating for more than 50 years and has become an institution in the city. You'll find anything from fairground-style rides like roller coasters, bumper cars, and carousels, through custom-made ghost towns. Expect plenty of food and drink stalls serving up U.S.- style cuisine including good old-fashioned hot dogs, hamburgers, and beer and ice cream.

DAHLEM & THE WEST

Club der Visionäre on the Spree River

For three days at the beginning of August, Berlin's east hosts the **Internationales Berliner Bierfestival** (International Beer Festival; *Karl-Marx-Allee, www.bierfestival-berlin.de*), drawing around 700,000 visitors from all over the world. Known as both the "beer mile" and the "longest beer garden in the world," the event showcases around 320 breweries from 86 countries. Take your pick from around 2,000 beer specialties.

■ OPEN-AIR CINEMA

A great way to spend an evening under the stars is to attend the **Freiluftkino** (Open-air Cinema; *www.freiluftkino-berlin.de, €€, May–Sept.*) in **Volkspark Friedrichshain** (see p. 128). Berliners come here to enjoy a nighttime movie with a bottle of wine and a picnic. You'll find a program of international movies, including some from February's **Berlinale** (see p. 102). A number of films are screened in English with German subtitles (check the cinema's website for details).

■ MUSIC EVENTS

At the end of June and for one night only, the **Waldbühne** (*Am Glockenturm, www.waldbuehne-berlin.de, 030 74 73 75 00, €€€€€*), a beautiful outdoor amphitheater in the woods at Dahlem, plays host to the **Berliner Philharmonie** for a themed festival of sounds that can range from Latin American rhythms to Tchaikovsky. It marks the end of the philharmonic's annual program.

In Kreuzberg, there is little to rival the charm of the canalside **Club der Visionäre** (*Am Flutgraben 2, www.clubdervisionaere.com, 030 69 51 89 42, €€*). Open year-round, this music venue comes into its own in summer. Listen to the club's evening program sitting beneath a huge weeping willow that overhangs waterfront decking.

A very different venue, for a few days each summer, Berlin's handsome

Gendarmenmarkt near Unter den Linden is transformed by **Classic Open Air** (*www.classicopenair.de, 030 31 57 54 0, €€€€€, early July*), a series of music events ranging from opera and operetta to pop, soul, and jazz.

In Berlin's east is **Mauerpark** (*Gleimstrasse 55, 030 60 98 00 18*), part of the so-called Death Strip that ran alongside the former Berlin Wall (the name means Wall Park). It is one of the district's most popular hangouts in summer, when lively karaoke sessions take place in the amphitheater, weather permitting.

■ Lange Nacht der Museen
The annual Long Night of Museums (*www.lange-nacht-der-museen.de, €€€€, Aug.*) involves some one hundred museums staying open way beyond their usual closing times. You'll have the opportunity to take a closer look at paintings, sculptures, and installations and watch a number of specially produced art performances, guided tours, and concerts. An information center at the **Kulturforum** (*Mattäikirchplatz 4–6, www.kultureforum-berlin.com, 030 26 62 1*) lists participating venues.

The bearpit karaoke sessions in Mauerpark are open to all aspiring stars of the stage.

PART 3

Travel Essentials

PLANNING YOUR TRIP

When to Go
Try as you will, there's no bad time to visit Berlin. The warm seasons are the obvious favorites for exploring the city on foot—spring, summer, and early fall. That said, the colder months offer many of the same world-class attractions.

To avoid the biggest crowds, enjoy a festival, and have a shot at decent weather, try visiting in the spring shoulder season from **April through early June,** or in the fall from **September to October.** Berlin's hectic pace slows a beat, hotels are cheaper, and lines shrink at the popular museums.

In the high-season months of **July and August,** Berlin crawls with tourists but on the upside, reliably balmy temperatures, beach bars, and a multitude of outdoor events will keep you smiling. In **December,** the Christmas markets spread a special magic, and some say you haven't lived until you pop the bubbly on New Year's Eve at the Brandenburg Gate.

Climate
Berlin's relatively cool, temperate climate has more in common with Moscow than Paris. Seasons are more extreme than the German average, with hot summers and fairly harsh winters. Cold fronts roll in from central Russia, bringing freezing temperatures and moderate, but usually not paralyzing, amounts of snow. In summer from June to late August, the mercury can soar into the low 90s°F (low 30s°C). Indian summer into late October can be delightful, with blue skies, fluffy clouds, and trees turning to gold.

Insurance
Take out enough travel insurance to cover emergency medical treatment, loss or theft, and repatriation.

Passports
U.S. and Canadian citizens can stay in Germany for up to three months with just a valid passport. No visa is required.

HOW TO GET TO BERLIN

By Airplane
There are surprisingly few direct flights to Berlin from outside Europe. Most arrivals are routed through larger European hubs in London, Amsterdam, or Frankfurt to board a connecting flight.

Until the new, much-delayed regional Berlin-Brandenburg Airport (BER) opens, possibly in 2016, flights will go in and out of two other airports, Tegel and Schönefeld. Some 5 miles (8 km) northwest of the center, **Tegel** links destinations within Germany and western Europe, while 11 miles (18 km) to the southeast of the city, **Schönefeld** serves the rest of the globe. Once BER opens, Tegel will be mothballed and Schönefeld absorbed.

For details of connections, contact the flight information desk *(01805 00 01 86)* or see the full schedule under Flight Planning *(www.berlin-airport.de).*

Both Schöneberg and Tegel are an easy train, bus, or taxi ride to/from downtown. Tegel is linked to the Hauptbahnhof (main train station, about 20 minutes) and Alexanderplatz (30 minutes) by the express TXL bus, and to Zoologischer Garten station (15 minutes) by Bus X9 or 109. Schönefeld is 30 to 45 minutes removed from Alexanderplatz by RE AirportExpress trains or by slower S-Bahn commuter rail.

A taxi from Tegel to Alexanderplatz will cost about €20 ($26); from Schönefeld it will run €30–€35 ($40–$45).

By Train
Germany's efficient national railway network is run by **Deutsche Bahn** (DB; *www .bahn.de).* Long-distance IntercityExpress (ICE), InterCity (IC), and EuroCity (EC) trains stop at both the main Hauptbahnhof and Ostbahnhof stations. RegionalExpress (RE) trains link Berlin to centers in the surrounding state of Brandenburg and beyond.

Every large station has a **Reisezentrum** (travel service center) with timetables and connections posted in the main hall. Train tickets are available at the service center, from DB vending machines, or online. If you wait to purchase your ticket on DB trains, you'll pay a surcharge. Foreign visitors are eligible for special vacation passes.

The **EurAide information center** (www.euraide.de) has an office in the first lower level of the Hauptbahnhof. Its English-speaking staff can handle complicated queries about train travel and itineraries.

By Bus
Slow but tolerably comfortable long-distance buses link Berlin to the rest of Europe. Most arrive at the ZOB (Zentraler Omnibusbahnhof; www.iob-berlin .de), the central bus station in Charlottenburg opposite the Funkturm (radio tower).

GETTING AROUND

Public Transportation
Berlin's tightly woven network of buses, trams (Strassenbahn), subways (U-Bahn), and commuter rail (S-Bahn) is run by the **Berlin Transport Authority BVG** (www.bvg.de, 030 19 44 9). U- and S-Bahns run from around 4 a.m. until 12:30–1:30 a.m., when night buses take over. On Fridays and Saturdays, U- and S-Bahns run all night.

Combined tickets are valid on buses, trams, and commuter rail. Buy tickets from ticket machines at U- or S-Bahn stops or, in the case of buses and trams, from the conductor or onboard ticket machine. Validate your ticket before traveling in a time-stamping machine—found inside buses and trams and on the station platforms. Failure to do so may incur a fine.

Berlin is divided into three public transportation zones: A and B for the central area, and C for outer districts, including Potsdam and Schönefeld Airport. Most destinations in town can be reached with an A-plus-B ticket.

Various tourist cards are available at ticket offices and many Berlin hotels. They include the **Berlin WelcomeCard,** a public transportation ticket valid for 48 hours, 72 hours, or five days on all buses, trams, and trains. Holders are entitled to free admission or reductions of up to 50 percent on guided tours or walks, boat trips, museums, theaters, and other leisure facilities in Berlin and Potsdam. The combined **Berlin WelcomeCard and Museum Island Pass** offers the same, but includes all sights on Museumsinsel, too.

By Bicycle
Berlin's growing network of bike paths is a serious alternative to road transportation and arguably the most pleasant and convenient way to get around.

The city has around 390 miles (620 km) of routes snaking through town and out into the countryside. A route map published by German cycling association **ADFC** (Brunnenstrasse 28, www.adfc.de, 030 448 47 24) is a good investment. You can plan urban journeys online at **BBBike** (www.bbbike.de), allowing you to set preferences for road type, greenery, and traffic lights.

If you take your bike on the train, buy an extra Fahrradkarte (bicycle ticket) and board carriages marked with a bicycle logo. You're not supposed to do so during peak times (6 a.m.– 9 a.m. and 2 p.m.–5 p.m. on weekdays), but officials turn a blind eye unless it's crowded.

Reliable bicycle agencies include **Prenzlberger Orange Bikes** (Kolle 37, www.kolle37.de, 030 44 35 68 52) and **Fat Tire** (under the Fernsehturm/TV Tower; www.berlinfahrradverleih .com, 030 24 04 79 91). An innovative rival is **Call-a-Bike** (www.callabike-interaktiv.de), whose fleet, available by the hour, day, or week, is positioned at nearly 100 stations in Mitte and Prenzlauer Berg.

By Taxi
Taxi stands are located at airports, at train and subway stations, and throughout the city, but you can also hail taxis in the street. Flag fall is €3.20 ($4.16), then €1.65 ($2.15) per km for the first 7 kilometers, then €1.28 ($1.66) per km after that. A tip for nightclubbers: a Kurzstrecke (short trip) up to 2 km (1.2 miles) costs €4 ($5.20)—inform the driver you want this fare before you set off.

By Train
For excursions farther afield, you'll need to take regional or national trains run by **Deutsche Bahn** (www.bahn.de). A private rail

operator, **Interconnex** *(www .interconnex.de)*, serves Leipzig and Schwerin and is usually cheaper than DB.

PRACTICAL ADVICE

Electricity
German circuits (mostly) use 220 volts. American appliances need adaptor plugs, and those that operate on 110 volts will also need a transformer.

Money Matters
The currency of Germany is the euro (€). There are 100 cents to 1 euro. Euro banknotes come in denominations of 5, 10, 20, 50, and 100, as well as the rare 200 and 500 bills. Coins come in €1 and €2 as well as 1, 2, 5, 10, 20, and 50 cents.

Most major banks have ATMs for bank cards and credit cards with instructions in several languages. Cash and traveler's checks can be exchanged in banks and currency booths at railroad stations and airports.

Opening Times
■ Banks: 8 a.m.–4 p.m. (around 5:30 p.m. on Thurs.); some in outlying areas close for lunch between 1 p.m. and 2 p.m. Closed Saturday and Sunday.
■ Museums: Generally 9 a.m.– 6 p.m. Many museums are closed on Monday but stay open late on Thursday evenings.
■ Pharmacies: Open during normal store hours and on a rotation schedule to cover nights and weekends.

■ Post Offices: Generally 8 a.m.–6 p.m. weekdays and until noon on Saturday.
■ Retailers: Weekdays 8:30 a.m.–6:30 p.m. (until 8 p.m. or 10 p.m. for many department stores and on Thursdays). On Saturday, hours are 8:30 a.m.– 8 p.m., although smaller shops close between noon and 2 p.m. Stores are generally closed on Sunday, except in airports and large train stations.

Post Offices
Post offices run by Deutsche Post, the national mail service, run like clockwork but are few and far between. Opening hours are generally 8 a.m. to 6 p.m. Monday to Friday and until noon on Saturday. Branches in airports and larger train stations are open seven days a week. Buy stamps at the post office counter or from vending machines outside. To find a post office branch near you, go to *www.deutschepost.de* and search under Filiale.

Telephones
Public telephones are available in ever dwindling numbers. The rate from telephone booths run by national provider Deutsche Telekom is about 23 cents a minute. Most public telephones are card operated, although some also take coins. Phone cards *(Telefonkarten)* are sold at post offices, convenience stores, and supermarkets for €10, €15, and €20. Note that numbers prefixed with 0900, 0180, or 0190 are toll numbers.

If you bring your cell phone to Germany, make sure it is compatible with Europe's GSM network. To keep costs down, sign up for an international roaming plan with your mobile provider. Or, once in Berlin you can a buy a local SIM card or inexpensive mobile with prepaid airtime. Check the offers at electronics warehouses like MediaMarkt or Saturn on Alexanderplatz.

Time Differences
Germany is on Central European Time (CET), six hours ahead of Eastern Standard Time. Noon in Germany is 6 a.m. in New York. Clocks move ahead one hour in the summer.

Travelers With Disabilities
There are access ramps and elevators in many public buildings, including train stations, museums, and theaters. Most buses and trams carry a blue wheelchair symbol and have special ramps. Most S- and U-Bahn stations downtown have ramps or elevators; exactly which ones do is displayed on the BVG network map. For information and support, contact the **Berlin Disabled Association** *(Jägerstrasse 63d, www.bbv-ev.de, 030 20 43 84 7)*. The online database of activist group **Mobidat** *(www.mobidat.net)* lists more than 34,000 buildings in Berlin, including hotels, restaurants, and cinemas, with details of their accessibility.

VISITOR INFORMATION

The city's tourist authority, **Berlin Tourism and Marketing** (BTM; www.visit berlin.de, 030 25 00 23 330) is helpful and well organized. A large Infostore is located in the Hauptbahnhof (8 a.m.–10 p.m. daily). You'll find branches in the south wing of the Brandenburg Gate, at the Alexa shopping mall on Alexanderplatz, in the Reichstag Pavilion, and at the airport.

EMERGENCIES

Crime and Police

Berlin is a remarkably safe place, and big-city common sense will steer you clear of most trouble. Some U- and S-Bahn stations in parts of Kreuzberg and Friedrichshain–Kottbusser Tor, Görlitzer Bahnhof, and Warschauer Strasse, for instance—may look rough, but the hang-abouts are generally harmless and looking for handouts. More care is urged in the outer suburbs of Lichtenberg, Marzahn, Neukölln, and Wedding, where muggings and street assaults do sometimes occur.

If you need help for any reason, dial emergency number 110 to contact the police. There are police stations in every district, including ones at Jägerstrasse 48 near Gendarmenmarkt and Joachimstaler Strasse 14–19 just south of Zoologischer Garten

station. The police will take a statement, cancel your credit cards, let you use the telephone, and help contact your embassy. If you encounter trouble on trains, the Bahnpolizei have offices at major stations.

German police officers can be identified by their solid blue uniforms (marked POLIZEI on the back) and blue-and-silver squad cars. Motorized police known as the Verkehrspolizei patrol the streets, roads, and motorways. Many German police officers speak English.

It is the law to carry proof of identification, such as a passport, driver's license, or ID card, with you at all times.

Embassies & Consulates

■ **British Embassy,** Wilhelmstrasse 70–71, www .ukingermany.fco.gov.uk, 030 20 45 70

■ **Canadian Embassy,** Leipziger Platz 17, 030 20 31 20

■ **U.S. Embassy,** American Citizen Services Section, Clayallee 170, www.germany .usembassy.gov, 030 83 05 0

Emergency Phone Numbers

■ Fire department & ambulance (Feuerwehr) 112
■ Police (Polizeinotruf) 110
■ Medical emergency (Notarzt, for house calls) 030 31 00 31
■ Dental emergency 030 89 00 43 33

Health

Apart from party fatigue, there are few health risks involved in visiting Berlin. For minor

ailments, qualified staff at pharmacies offer expert advice. Doctors' consulting hours are normally 9 a.m. to noon and 3 to 5 p.m., except weekends. For urgent attention outside consulting hours, go to a hospital (Krankenhaus). German medical treatment and facilities are generally very good. The best known hospital in Berlin is the **Charité** (Schumannstrasse 20–21, 030 450 50), which has a 24-hour emergency ward.

Lost Property

Your travel insurance should cover the loss or theft of your property if you are not already covered by your home insurance. Theft must be reported to the police so you can obtain a certificate confirming that the crime has been reported. The national rail service, Deutsche Bahn, has its own lost property office (0900 19 90 59 9), as does the Berlin urban transportation network BVG (030 19 44 9). For items lost elsewhere, try the municipal lost property office (Fundbüro, Potsdamer Strasse 180/182, 030 19 44 9).

Lost/Stolen Credit Cards

■ American Express (AE), www.americanexpress.com, 069 97 97 20 00
■ Diners Club (DC), www .dinersclub.com, 07531 363 31 11
■ MasterCard (MC), www .mastercard.com, 0800 819 10 40
■ Visa (V), www.visa.com, 0800 811 84 40

HOTELS

Berlin has plenty of guest beds: more than 130,000 at last count. This is an investment in the future and good news for visitors. The excess capacity translates into rates well below those in, say, Amsterdam, London, or Paris. This is a fairly compact city, so you should be able to find a hotel within a reasonable distance of the sights. Remember that Berlin is a major destination for its clubbing scene, and Berliners traditionally stay out long into the night, particularly on weekends, so you may prefer a room facing away from main roads. Many hotels accept all major cards, although some of the smaller hotels take only cash.

TRAVEL ESSENTIALS

A spree of hotel-building has brought eastern Berlin largely up to standards in the west of the city. The central Mitte district boasts the lion's share of main draws such as the Museum Island art collections, and naturally it's the most popular area to stay. The old West can feel a bit staid, but there's refined charm in the squares and boutique-lined streets that feed into Kurfürstendamm (Ku'damm).

Before you book a room, it helps to make a personal checklist of must-have features such as elevators, air-conditioning, or a quiet location. Many hotels overlook busy streets, and not all have decent soundproofing.

If you're driving, know that many central hotels do not have their own parking and may direct you to a paid lot or garage nearby. Street parking may be tricky in built-up areas, although some establishments in the city issue permits.

In our listings, unless otherwise stated:
• Breakfast is not included in the price.
• All rooms have a telephone and television. Many hotels

also provide Internet access, and Wi-Fi is standard in mid-to top-end establishments.
• Room prices are a rough indicator and do not take seasonal variations or special offers into account.

Online Resources: A good starting point is www.visit berlin.de, run by the city's capable tourist authority, Berlin Tourismus Marketing. The search-and-book pages show availability, special offers, location, features, and photos for more than 400 hotels, hostels, and B&Bs.

Price Range

An indication of the cost of a double room in the high season is given by € signs.
€€€€€ More than €200
€€€€ €150–€200
€€€ €100–€150
€€ €60–€100
€ Less than €60

Text Symbols
🛏 No. of Guest Rooms
🚇 U-Bahn or S-Bahn 🅿 Parking
⤴ Elevator ❄ Air-conditioning
🚭 Nonsmoking 🏊 Outdoor Pool
🏊 Indoor Pool 💪 Health Club
💳 Credit Cards

Organization

Hotels listed here have been grouped first according to neighborhood, then listed alphabetically by price range.

UNTER DEN LINDEN & AROUND

Some of Berlin's most impressive luxury hotels are to be found in this neighborhood, as well as rooms for those on more modest budgets. This is a good location for all the major sights in central Berlin, including Potsdamer Platz with a range of attractions day and night. A number of these hotels are also perfectly placed for the government quarter and Tiergarten Park.

■ **GRAND HYATT**
€€€€€
MARLENE-DIETRICH-PLATZ 2
TEL 030 25 53 12 34
www.berlin.hyatt.com
A haunt of movie stars, celebrities, and the merely moneyed, this temple of luxury has matte black surfaces and carved cedarwood that exude a Euro-Japanese elegance. Rooms boast amenities such as heated bathroom floors and

Bauhaus art. On the rooftop you'll find a gym, pool, and beauty center.

ⓘ *342* 🚇 *S1, S2, U2 Potsdamer Platz* 🅿 🔄 🛇 🛋 📶
🛇 *All major cards*

■ **HOTEL ADLON KEMPINSKI**
€€€€€
UNTER DEN LINDEN 77
TEL 030 22 61 11 11
www.hotel-adlon.de
British club meets art deco at this portal of German history, where Marlene Dietrich was discovered and Joseph Goebbels chased his mistress down the corridor. The grand dame of Berlin hotels has been restored to its pre–World War II splendor, complete with grandstand views of the Brandenburg Gate, not only from a number of the rooms, but also from terraced seating outside. The elegant Lorenz restaurant boasts three Michelin stars. All rooms have flatscreen TVs and Wi-Fi.

ⓘ *382 + suites* 🚇 *U55, S1, S2 Brandenburger Tor* 🅿 🔄 🛇 🛋 📶 🛇 *All major cards*

■ **RITZ-CARLTON BERLIN**
€€€€€
POTSDAMER PLATZ 3
TEL 030 33 77 77
www.ritzcarlton.com
One of Berlin's premier luxury hotels, housed in a retro U.S.-style skyscraper with a hushed, columned lobby and sweeping staircase that harks back to the Prussian Empire. Rooms gleam with polished cherrywood, marble, and brass fittings. The

Curtain Club resembles a British gentlemen's club, complete with fireplace. To add to the ambience, the bar curtains are ceremoniously raised every night by a genuine beefeater.

ⓘ *341 + suites* 🚇 *S2, S2, U2 Potsdamer Platz* 🅿 🔄 🛇 🛋
🛇 *All major cards*

■ **SOFITEL GENDARMENMARKT**
€€€€
CHARLOTTENSTRASSE 50–52
TEL 030 20 37 50
www.dorint.com
A major facelift turned this ex-communist hotel on Gendarmenmarkt, a gorgeous church-studded square, into a cozy retreat. Light floods into the atrium restaurant, the rooftop gym, and even the ballroom via translucent floor tiles. Rooms are on the snug side but comfortable, and the upper-floor balconies are level with the stunning belfry of the Französischer Dom.

ⓘ *114* 🚇 *U2 Stadtmitte* 🅿 🔄 🛇 🛋 📶 🛇 *All major cards*

■ **MANDALA SUITES**
€€€–€€€€
FRIEDRICHSTRASSE 185–190
TEL 030 20 29 20
www.themandala.de
All manner of sophisticates frequent this ultra-discreet hideaway on Friedrichstrasse. If you want room service and bellboys go someplace else, but you'll miss being pampered in five categories of suite ranging from 430 to 1,100 square feet (40–100 sq m). Rooms have marble baths, walk-in closets, kitchen, and modern

workspaces with Wi-Fi.

ⓘ *82 suites* 🚇 *U2, U6 Stadtmitte* 🅿 🔄 🛇 📶
🛇 *All major cards*

AROUND MUSEUMSINSEL

This neighborhood offers a good range of hotels in the vibrant heart of the city. You won't improve on location when it comes to sightseeing: Museumsinsel, piers on the Spree River, and Alexanderplatz are all within minutes on foot. There are good shopping opportunities, too, at Friedrichstrasse and the Hackesche Höfe. This is, however, a busy district and can be noisy come nighttime.

■ **ART'OTEL BERLIN**
€€€€
WALLSTRASSE 70–73
TEL 030 24 06 20
www.artotels.de
This rococo mansion, a onetime haunt of Berlin's intellectual elite, is now a plush hotel cum art gallery. Spread over its six floors is a collection of works by modernist painter Georg Baselitz. You can dine in the glass-roofed Factory restaurant or outside on the banks of the Spree River.

ⓘ *105* 🚇 *U2 Märkisches Museum* 🅿 🔄 🛇 🛋
🛇 *All major cards*

■ **RADISSON SAS**
€€€–€€€€
KARL-LIEBKNECHT-STRASSE 3
TEL 030 23 82 80
www.radissonsas.com

HOTELS

The Radisson claims the world's largest cylindrical aquarium (82 ft/25 m high) and most guests fall under its Jules Verne spell right away. The most impressive rooms face either the towering tank in the atrium-style lobby or overlook the Spree River and majestic Berlin Cathedral. Flatscreen TVs and free Wi-Fi are standard. All guests get a free riverboat tour, and for those with energy to burn, the fitness room is open 24 hours.

ⓘ 427 🚇 S5, S7, U2, U5, U8 Alexanderplatz 🅿 ♿ 🍴 📶 ☕ 🍸 💳 All major cards

■ ALEXANDER PLAZA
€€€
ROSENSTRASSE 1
TEL 030 24 00 17 63
www.hotel-alexander-plaza.de

Housed in a stolid Bismarck-era monument that was once a furrier's studio, this hotel bristles with period details. There are vintage glazed tiles and a "floating" staircase apparently held up by stucco. The ergonomically designed rooms have soothing color schemes and panoramas of the historic quarter. Breakfast is served in the glass-covered Wintergarten.

ⓘ 92 🚇 S5, S7, U2, U5, U8 Alexanderplatz 🅿 ♿ 📶 🍸 💳 All major cards

■ ARCOTEL VELVET
€€€
ORANIENBURGER STRASSE 52
TEL 030 278 75 30
www.arcotel.at

This stylish member of the Arcotel chain occupies a plum spot in Mitte, close to the Neue Synagoge and Friedrichstrasse. Furnishings are sleek contemporary with dark hardwoods, red leather, and floor-to-ceiling windows. Flatscreen TVs and free room Wi-Fi are standard. Rooms on the upper floors offer fabulous views over the historic district. Breakfast is served in the fine Lutter & Wegner restaurant.

ⓘ 85 🚇 U6 Oranienburger Tor 🅿 ♿ 📶 📶 💳 All major cards

■ ARTIST RIVERSIDE
€€€
FRIEDRICHSTRASSE 106
TEL 030 28 49 00
www.great-hotel.de

Behind its bland communist-era facade, you'll be surprised by the quirky blend of art nouveau decor and spa reception. Rooms range from basic budget to the pleasure-filled suite with waterbed and a claw-footed tub. Vegas-style highlight: a spa with shell-shaped saltwater tub for two. Windows in many rooms, as well as the downstairs café and restaurant, have arresting views over the Spree.

ⓘ 40 🚇 S1, S2, S5, S7, U6 Friedrichstrasse 🅿 ♿ 📶 🍸 💳 All major cards

■ THE DUDE
€€€
KÖPENICKER STRASSE 92
TEL 030 41 19 88 17 7
www.thedudeberlin.com

Housed in one of historic Berlin's oldest surviving buildings (1822), this designer hotel exudes an atmosphere of staying in one's own private luxury residence. The hotel has a range of rooms with flawless attention to detail and exquisite modern furniture. Features include a cigar lounge and welcome wine and candy with every room. The in-house restaurant, The Brooklyn, is renowned for its steaks and 160 rare whiskies.

ⓘ 30 🚇 U2 Märkisches Museum 🅿 📶 ♿ All major cards

■ HACKESCHER MARKT
€€€
GROSSE PRÄSIDENTENSTRASSE 8
TEL 030 28 00 30
www.hotel-hackescher-markt
.com

In a nicely renovated 19th-century town house, this urbane hotel is perfectly situated for tapping the nightlife around Hackescher Markt. The rooms and suites have pleasant country-style furnishings and floor heating in the bathrooms. Most quarters face a peaceful green courtyard, and some even have balconies. The English-speaking staff are eager to help. Although some rooms are snug, you can't quibble with the location.

ⓘ 31 + 3 suites 🚇 S5, S7, Hackescher Markt 🅿 ♿ 📶 All major cards

■ HONIGMOND GARDEN
€€€
INVALIDENSTRASSE 122
TEL 030 28 44 55 77
www.honigmond.de

This romantic, family-run hotel transports you to 19th-century Berlin with original antiques, stucco

TRAVEL ESSENTIALS

ceilings, and polished wood floors. The rear chambers and kitchen-equipped cottages face an idyllic, shady garden with Japanese fishpond and century-old trees. Breakfast is included in the price.

ⓘ 20 **🚉** S1, S2 Nordbahnhof **P** **Ⓢ** **Ⓐ** No credit cards

■ INDIGO
€€€
BERNHARD-WEISS-STRASSE 5
TEL 030 505 08 60
www.hotelindigoberlin.com
Located just a few minutes' walk north of Alexanderplatz, this new and affordable hotel is a good home base for exploring central Berlin. The rooms are small but crisply clean and modern, and excellent service is provided by a friendly, youthful staff. Other amenities include a large and welcoming bar, free Wi-Fi, in-room coffee machines, and a well-appointed gym.

ⓘ 153 **🚉** S5, S7, U2, U5, U8 Alexanderplatz **P** (in vicinity) **⊟** **Ⓢ** **📺** **Ⓐ** All major cards

■ KÜNSTLERHEIM LUISE
€€€
LUISENSTRASSE 19
TEL 030 28 44 80
www.kuenstlerheim-luise.de
Bedroom fantasy, you say? Each of the 50 rooms at this wacky art hotel is an installation designed by young artists. Some play with your head (one has a ridiculously huge four-poster bed), draw on sci-fi (a Jetsons shower), or are chilled (Japanese screens and Zen music). The location is convenient to the Reichstag,

Unter den Linden, and the sights along Oranienburger Strasse. Rooms are tastefully appointed and quiet, apart from a few bedrooms next to the S-Bahn tracks.

ⓘ 50 **🚉** U6 Oranienburger Tor; S1, S2, S5, S7, U6 Friedrichstrasse **⊟** **Ⓢ** **🏊** **📺** **Ⓐ** All major cards

■ LUX ELEVEN
€€€
ROSA-LUXEMBURG-STRASSE 9–13
TEL 030 936 28 00
www.lux-eleven.com
A haunt of pencil-thin fashion models and media types, these spacious apartments were once used by visitors to the dreaded Ministry of State Security. They are now done up in a minimalist Far Eastern style. Soft cuddly things abound—pillows, comfy chairs, piles of towels—to make spaces plush and inviting. Rooms boast Wi-Fi and flatscreen TVs. Guests here can plug into the gallery scene of Mitte or just retreat to their personal cocoons.

ⓘ 72 apts. **🚉** S5, S7, U2, U5, U8 Alexanderplatz **P** **⊟** **Ⓢ** **📺** **Ⓐ** All major cards

■ MONBIJOU HOTEL
€€€
MONBIJOUPLATZ 1
TEL 030 61 62 03 00
www.monbijouhotel.com
Steps from Hackescher Markt, this stylish boutique features plush modern decor with hardwood floors, a well-stocked library, and large windows overlooking the Mitte neighborhood—some with obstructed views of Berliner Dom. There's a pleasant bar

area and lounge with fireplace, and the Parisian-style bistro offers an international menu. In summer enjoy snacks and drinks on the rooftop terrace.

ⓘ 101 **🚉** S5, S7 Hackescher Markt **P** (fee) **⊟** **Ⓢ** **Ⓐ** All major cards

■ THE CIRCUS HOTEL
€€–€€€
ROSENTHALER STRASSE 108005
TEL 030 20 00 39 39
www.circus-berlin.de
The Circus is handily situated on Rosenthaler Platz in the hub of the Mitte district. The garden courtyard (and rear quarters overlooking it) are a great place to relax, and there are hip little amenities such as iPods loaded with Berlin music. Rooms are clean, stylish, and sport imaginative touches—look for the quotes engraved in windows. There's Wi-Fi throughout, and all of the rooms have laptop safes.

ⓘ 60 **🚉** U8 Rosenthaler Platz **⊟** **Ⓢ** **Ⓐ** All major cards

■ BERLIN APARTMENT
€€
VETERANENSTRASSE 10
TEL 030 70 22 13 58
www.midi-inn.de
This stylish boutique hotel has an enviable location—overlooking the rolling Weinbergspark, on the cusp of sight-filled Mitte and hip Prenzlauer Berg. Though on the cozy side, the double rooms have huge windows, smart designs, and attractive canvases by a London artist. Management rents out several fine apartments close

by. Breakfast is served in the Mediterranean restaurant-bar.

ⓘ *3 + 4 apts.* 🚇 *U8 Rosenthaler Platz* ⊟ ⓢ
🏧 *AE, MC, V*

■ WOMBAT'S CITY

€

ALTE SCHÖNHAUSER STRASSE 2
TEL 030 84 71 08 20
www.wombats-hostels.com
Run by a young, go-ahead staff of expats in a vibrant neighborhood, the Wombat nicely combines a kicking party hostel with hotel amenities. Rates in the spotless, three- to six-bed dorms include bedsheets, kitchen use, and Web access in the downstairs lounge. Double rooms are available—a real deal in this category. The popular rooftop bar affords a stunning view over Mitte, and several nightclubs are within walking distance.

ⓘ *84 + 4 apts.* 🚇 *U2 Rosa-Luxemburg-Platz* ⊟ ⓢ
🏧 *AE, MC, V*

TIERGARTEN & AROUND

This is one of Berlin's quieter neighborhoods. Hotels here are perfectly placed for visiting the government quarter, the diplomatic quarter, and, of course, Berlin's green lung, Tiergarten Park. A number of hotels are also within walking distance of the Kulturforum to the south of the park, for art galleries by day and the Berlin Philharmonie by night.

■ DAS STUE

€€€–€€€€

DRAKESTRASSE 1
TEL 030 31 17 22 0
www.das-stue.com
Claiming to be Berlin's first luxury boutique hotel, Das Stue nestles in lush Tiergarten park, close to Berlin's zoological gardens. The handsome 1930s building—originally the Danish Embassy—has been remodeled within by Spanish architect Patricia Urquiola. The generous rooms are luxurious and come with all modern comforts, including free Wi-Fi. The hotel has two restaurants, one of which (Cinco) is Michelin-starred.

ⓘ *70* 🚇 *S5, S7 Tiergarten* ⓟ ⊟
ⓢ 🛏 📶 🏧 *All major cards*

■ ABION SPREEBOGEN WATERSIDE HOTEL

€€–€€€

ALT-MOABIT 99
TEL 030 39 92 09 90
www.abion-hotel.de
Towering above the Spree River north of Tiergarten park, this hotel is housed in a former dairy farm. With its own landing pier right outside, the hotel runs a number of river cruises. There are several well-appointed family rooms and suites available. You'll pay more for a riverside room—which comes with free refreshments, slippers, and bathrobes—but the views are worth it. Additional features include an in-house restaurant, bicycle rental, and free Wi-Fi.

ⓘ *238 + 19 suites* 🚇 *U9 Turmstrasse* ⊟ ⓢ 📶
🏧 *All major cards*

■ BERLIN, BERLIN

€€–€€€

LÜTZOWPLATZ 17
TEL 030 260 50
www.hotel-berlin-berlin.com
Host to many a business conference, this cavernous hotel has more than 700 rooms, yet manages to feel warm and personal. During the Cold War, visiting celebrities and politicians often stayed here, and staff are full of anecdotes of the era. The rooms are immense, modern, and spotless. Wi-Fi is free throughout the hotel, and breakfast is included.

ⓘ *710* 🚇 *U1, U3, U4 Nollendorfplatz* ⓟ ⊟ ⓢ 📶
🏧 *All major cards*

CHARLOTTENBURG

This well-established neighborhood was the hub of West Berlin during the Cold War. It is the ideal location from which to visit Charlottenburg Palace and remains one of Berlin's principle shopping districts. Hotels here are good value for money on the whole, and there are plenty of restaurants to choose from in the streets around Savignyplatz, Breitscheidplatz, and Kurfürstendamm.

■ BRANDENBURGER HOF

€€€€€

EISLEBENER STRASSE 14
TEL 030 21 40 50
www.brandenburger-hof.com
Bauhaus and modern design come together in this elegant villa dating from the early

1900s. The hotel is supremely atmospheric and quiet, featuring stylish but livable rooms with 13-foot (4 m) ceilings. The house restaurant, Die Quadriga, is considered one of the city's finest and serves only fine German wines.

ℹ 58 **🚇** U3 Augsburger Strasse **P** 🔁 🎱 🅂 🍷
🃏 All major cards

■ Q!
€€€–€€€€
KNESEBECKSTRASSE 67
TEL 030 810 06 60
www.loock-hotels.com
A cool gray facade signals your arrival at the Q!, an ultrachic retreat named for the nearby Ku'damm. This hotel smoothes out the rough edges by eliminating corners. Hardwood floors curve up the walls in the rooms, where you can literally slide from the tub into bed. The spa has its own self-contained beach with heated sand, aromatherapy, and sound and light effects.

ℹ 77 **🚇** S5, S7 Savignyplatz **P**
🅂 🍷 🃏 All major cards

■ SAVOY
€€€–€€€€
FASANENSTRASSE 9–10
TEL 030 31 10 30
www.hotel-savoy.com
A Berlin institution, this hotel oozes an old-world charm of bowler hats and rustling petticoats. Standard rooms are a little generic, while the suites on the air-conditioned sixth floor—named after regulars like Henry Miller or Greta Garbo—have heaps of character.

The Times Bar has a walk-in humidor.

ℹ 125 **🚇** S5, S7, U2 Zoologischer Garten, U9 🔁 🎱 🅂
🃏 All major cards

■ BLEIBTREU
€€€
BLEIBTREUSTRASSE 31
TEL 030 88 47 40
www.bleibtreu.com
The cheery, ecofriendly materials and minimalist Italian furniture of this boutique hotel are completely in step with the fancy apparel shops along Bleibtreustrasse. Some of the rooms are on the tight side, but the in-house bar and Restaurant 31 are quite elegant.

ℹ 59 **🚇** S5, S7, S9 Savignyplatz; U1 Uhlandstrasse, U9 🔁 🅂 🍷
🃏 All major cards

■ CASA
€€€
SCHLÜTERSTRASSE 40
TEL 030 280 30 00
www.hotel-casa.de
This slick hotel caters to savvy urbanites who value practical but chic decor. The color schemes meld designer cool and welcoming hospitality. The sleek Philippe Starck furniture is offset by warm Mediterranean hues in the roomy apartments. Breakfast is served until noon.

ℹ 29 **🚇** S5, S7, S9 Savignyplatz; U1 Uhlandstrasse, U9 🔁 🅂
🃏 All major cards

■ HECKER'S
€€€
GROLMANSTRASSE 35
TEL 030 889 00
www.heckers-hotel.de

Just a few steps off busy Kurfürstendamm, this renowned boutique hotel prides itself on the personal service it heaps on celebrities that have included Michael Douglas, Valéry Giscard d'Estaing, and Austrian rock star Udo Jürgens. The huge, elegant quarters range from Bauhaus to Italo-chic. The lobby has a striking ice blue backlit bar.

ℹ 72 **🚇** U1 Uhlandstrasse **P**
🔁 🎱 🅂 🃏 All major cards

■ KU'DAMM 101
€€€
KURFÜRSTENDAMM 101
TEL 030 520 05 50
www.kudamm101.com
A bit removed from the action, this hotel is fascinating viewing for anyone with an eye for minimalist design. The lobby combines 1960s' design with New Age—column lamps, curvy banquettes, and recessed ceilings. The rooms are a clever blend of light and shadow. There's high-speed Internet and retro touches like a wood-grain console that hides the TV.

ℹ 1&0 **🚇** S41, S42, S47 Halensee **P** 🔁 🅂
🃏 All major cards

■ ASKANISCHER HOF
€€–€€€
KURFÜRSTENDAMM 53
TEL 030 881 80 33
www.askanischer-hof.de
For a dose of Berlin history, check into this intimate hotel on the city's most famous shopping avenue. The Askanischer Hof was raised in the early 1900s and furnished

in Golden 1920s style. The rooms are all individually designed and boast high-tech features. Rock star David Bowie was a regular guest in the 1970s.

ⓘ 16 🚇 S5, S7 Savignyplatz
🅿 ♨ ⬣ All major cards

■ BIKINI 25 HOURS
€€–€€€
BUDAPESTER STRASSE 40
TEL 030 12 02 21 0
www.25hours-hotels.com
This hotel is arguably Berlin's hippest new arrival. With "urban jungle" as their theme, the hotel's rooms are divided into those that look out across the city (Urban) and those that overlook the ape house at Berlin's zoo (Jungle). The hotel also boasts a wood-fire bakery, sauna, and roof terrace with views across Tiergarten park. Free bike rental and Wi-Fi come as standard with every room.

ⓘ 149 🚇 S5, S7, U1, U2, U9 Zoologischer Garten ⬌ ⬣
⬣ No credit cards

■ PENSION DITTBERNER
€€–€€€
WIELANDSTRASSE 26
TEL 030 884 69 50
www.hotel-dittberner.de
This friendly third-floor pension has been in the Lange family for generations. This is old Berlin in spades: soaring ceilings, adorned with stucco and aging lithographs, and a bright breakfast room with antique sideboard. Breakfast is included.

ⓘ 22 🚇 S5, S7, S9 Savignyplatz 🅿 ⬌ ⬣
⬣ No credit cards

■ PROPELLER ISLAND CITY LODGE
€€–€€€
ALBRECHT-ACHILLES-STRASSE 58
TEL 030 891 90 16
www.propeller-island.com
Get ready for a surprise—nothing about this place can be described as ordinary. This 19th-century apartment block has been rewired as an eccentric hotel where every room is an inhabitable work of art. Beds can be found in coffins, hovering in the air, or hidden in a fortress. The Two Lions sports a pair of caged mattresses 5 feet (1.5 m) above the ground. Every stick of furniture was designed and crafted by the owner-artist himself.

ⓘ 45 🚇 U7 Adenauerplatz
⬣ No credit cards

BERLIN'S EAST

Berlin's eastern districts offer accommodations in the leafy residential streets of Prenzlauer Berg as well as close proximity to the clubbing scene in Friedrichshain. The area has a relatively laid-back vibe with a lively café and restaurant scene. However, with the exception of the Berlin Wall Memorial and the East Side Gallery, none of the city's major sights are in this area.

■ NHOW BERLIN
€€€–€€€€
STRALAUER ALLEE 3
TEL 030 290 29 90
www.nhow-hotels.com
Flash Gordon meets Barbie at

this "music lifestyle hotel" lodged in a converted riverside granary. Futuristic shapes and bubblegum colors are dominant themes. All rooms are equipped with Wi-Fi, iPod dock, and flatscreen IP-TVs that double as mirrors. The stainless-steel tower has a number of music studios for rent; room service will even send up a Gibson guitar with headphones.

ⓘ 304 🚇 S5, S7, U1 Warschauer Strasse 🅿 ⬌ ⬣ ⬣
♨ ⬣ All major cards

■ ADELE
€€€
GREIFSWALDER STRASSE 227
TEL 030 44 32 43 10
www.adele-hotel.de
From the street, this lounge hotel is cleverly camouflaged by a row of coffee and wine shops. Rooms look like something out of *Wallpaper* magazine, with dark hardwoods and leathers set off by cream and pastel hues. There's a fine Mediterranean-inspired restaurant.

ⓘ 14 🚇 U2 Senefelderplatz
🅿 ⬌ ⬣ ⬣ All major cards

■ KASTANIENHOF
€€€
KASTANIENALLEE 65
TEL 030 44 30 50
www.kastanienhof.biz
This guesthouse has a great location on Kastanienallee, a hip nightlife strip in Prenzlauer Berg. The historic building hosted a butcher shop, Russian military post, and tenements before being turned into one of East Berlin's first hotels after reunification. The furnishings are simple, but the historic

TRAVEL ESSENTIALS

maps and photos in the rooms ooze atmosphere.

1 35 **▦** U8 Rosenthaler Platz
P **⊜** **⊗** **⊛** All major cards

■ MICHELBERGER
€€–€€€
WARSCHAUER STRASSE 39
TEL 030 29 77 85 90
FAX 934 881 880
www.michelbergerhotel.com
An old warehouse reborn as a hotel, the Michelberger pitches affordable charms for night owls in buzzing Friedrichshain. The interiors of this budget boutique hotel are kept raw with exposed wiring, feature playful touches like raised beds, and have free Wi-Fi. The laid-back bar area has comfy sofas and a travel library that is well worth a browse. This hotel is within easy walking distance of some of Europe's best nightclubs, including Berghain.

1 119 **▦** S5, S7, U1 Warschauer Strasse **⊜** **⊗** **⊛** MC, V

■ ALTE-BÄCKEREI-PANKOW
€€
WOLLANKSTRASSE 130
TEL 030 293 750
www.alte-baeckerei-pankow.de
This has to be one of the quaintest places to stay in Berlin. Occupying the attic rooms of an old bakery, this pension sleeps just four people. With rustic furnishings throughout, its rooms are reminiscent of scenes from Hansel and Gretel or Goldilocks. Also on the premises are a museum of childhood and a fully

operational bakery, producing rustic-looking bread (3–8 p.m., Tues., Wed., Fri.).

1 2 **▦** S2, S8, U1 Pankow
P **⊗** **⊛** No credit cards

■ EAST SIDE
€€
MÜHLENSTRASSE 6
TEL 030 29 38 34 00
www.eastsidehotel.de
A stone's throw from the East Side Gallery—the longest remaining section of the Berlin Wall—this friendly, supermodern hotel has a minimalist decor featuring art and photos devoted to the former barrier. Front rooms have views of the gallery and the Spree River but are noisier than those to the rear. Breakfast is included and served 24 hours.

1 36 **▦** S5, S7, U1 Warschauer Strasse **P** **⊜**
⊛ All major cards

■ 26 BERLIN
€€
GRÜNBERGER STRASSE 26
TEL 030 297 77 80
www.hotel26-berlin.de
For no-nonsense digs a cut above a hostel, try this small, eco-friendly hotel in the go-ahead Friedrichshain district. Breakfast (included) is a magnificent organic spread of cheeses, fresh juices, and cold cuts. You can chill in the pleasant café or catch some rays on the lounge chairs in the rear garden.

1 19 **▦** S5, S7, U1 Warschauer Strasse
P **⊗**
⊛ All major cards

■ UPSTALSBOOM
€€
GUBENER STRASSE 42
TEL 030 293 750
www.upstalsboom-berlin.de
An oddity in landlocked Berlin, this perky hotel is part of a chain of seaside resorts. The sleek rooms come in four sizes, some with kitchens, and the Friesendeel restaurant serves wonderful fish specialties. The rooftop garden has sweeping views over the Friedrichshain district. Rates include bicycle rentals and use of the sauna and gym.

1 170 **▦** S5, S7, U1 Warschauer Strasse **P** **⊜** **⊗** **▯**
⊛ All major cards

■ GREIFSWALD
€–€€
GREIFSWALDER STRASSE 211
TEL 030 442 78 88
www.hotel-greifswald.de
Tucked into a historic building, this little hotel is something of a rock shrine. Guests have included members of Steppenwolf and guitarist Albert Lee. Dozens of autographed photos adorn the reception area and breakfast room. The comfy, albeit generic, rooms and small apartments with kitchen are popular with families.

1 30 **▦** Tram M4 or Bus 200
P **⊗** **⊛** All major cards

■ JUNCKER'S
€–€€
GRÜNBERGER STRASSE 21
TEL 030 293 35 50
www.junckers-hotel.de
This family-run hotel is one of Berlin's best kept secrets.

The simple rooms are cut a little close but are bright and spotless. Free Wi-Fi, coffee, and mineral water make you feel right at home. The gracious owner, Herr Juncker, is a font of local knowledge.

🚪 30 🚇 S5, S7, S9, U1 *Warschauer Strasse* 🅿 ⬍
♿ *MC, V*

SCHÖNEBERG & KREUZBERG

With a sprinkling of major sights that include the Jüdisches Museum, the Berlinische Galerie, and the Landwehrkanal, these neighborhoods combine the quiet, leafy streets of bohemian Schöneberg with the more multicultual, edgy vibe of Kreuzberg and Kottbusser Tor. Now stretching toward up-and-coming Neukölln, this district has plenty of good-value accommodations and a rich and varied nightlife.

■ HÜTTENPALAST BERLIN
€€€
HOBRECHTSTRASSE 66
TEL 030 37 30 58 06
www.huettenpalast.de
Indoor "glamping" is the draw at this old vacuum cleaner factory. Artists have redesigned three vintage camping trailers and three huts for guests. Relax in the garden under fake trees. An organic breakfast (included) is served in the courtyard café. Regular rooms with en suite bathrooms are available in the rear wing.

🚪 19 🚇 U7, U8 *Hermannplatz*

■ MÖEVENPICK BERLIN
€€€
SCHÖNEBERGER STRASSE 3
TEL 030 23 00 60
www.moevenpickhotels.com
Once the headquarters of electronics giant Siemens, this hotel south of Potsdamer Platz offers funky design in a historic shell. The lounge bar is made of high-voltage equipment, and old turbines are displayed in the halls. Other highlights are the glass-bricked bathrooms, olivewood, and perky colors recalling Möevenpick ice cream.

🚪 243 🚇 S1, S2 *Anhalter Bahnhof* 🅿 ⬍ ♿ 🔲 🍴
♿ *All major cards*

■ RIEHMERS
€€€
YORCKSTRASSE 83
TEL 030 78 09 88 00
www.riehmers-hofgarten.de
This romantic small hotel near Viktoriapark was designed by Wilhelm Riehmer, a talented 19th-century architect. French double doors open into spacious rooms with stucco ceilings and contemporary décor. The in-house restaurant, named for writer E. T. A. Hoffmann, serves meals in a quiet cobblestone courtyard.

🚪 22 🚇 U6, U7 *Mehringdamm*
🅿 ⬍ ♿ *All major cards*

■ PARK PLAZA WALL STREET
€€–€€€
WALLSTRASSE 23–24
TEL 030 847 11 70
www.parkplaza.com
This deluxe four-star hotel near Checkpoint Charlie is something of a capitalist send-up, with dollar bills and stock-ticker symbols printed on carpets and drapes. The quarters are plush, and state of the art. The well-appointed rooms are packed with quality woods, textiles, and perks like free Wi-Fi, a flatscreen TV, and a laptop safe.

🚪 80 🚇 U2 *Märkisches Museum*
🅿 ⬍ ♿ 🔲 🍴
♿ *All major cards*

DAHLEM & THE WEST

Merely a fifteen-minute ride to central Berlin on the S-Bahn, this neighborhood feels a world apart from the inner city. You'll find exceptional value for money and simple comfort in streets lined with 19th-century villas. Close proximity to Grunewald, the Dahlem Museums, and Berlin's botanical gardens.

■ HOTEL FRIEDENAU
€–€€
FREGESTRASSE 68
TEL 030 85 90 96 0
www.literaturhotel-berlin.de
This elegant 19th-century villa is furnished in the German Biedermeier style. At the heart of the hotel is a room dedicated to the area's literary heroes, with books, biographies, manuscripts, drawings, and photos. In summer, you can breakfast in the dappled shade of the garden to the rear of the hotel.

🚪 17 🚇 S1 *Friedenau*
🅿 ⬍ ♿ *V, MC*

LANGUAGE **GUIDE**

In German "ss" can also be written as "ß." Called a "sharp s," you will see this construction in many words, such as *Straße* (street). It is pronounced in exactly the same way as "ss."

Useful Words & Phrases
Yes *Ja*
No *Nein*
Please *Bitte*
Thank you *Danke*
Excuse me *Entschuldigen Sie bitte*
Goodbye *Auf Wiedersehen*
Good morning *Guten Morgen*
Good day (afternoon) *Guten Tag*
Good evening *Guten Abend*
Good night *Gute Nacht*
today *heute*
yesterday *gestern*
tomorrow *morgen*
now *jetzt*
later *später*
left *links*
right *rechts*
straight ahead *geradeaus*
Do you speak English? *Sprechen Sie Englisch?*
I am American *Ich bin Amerikaner (m)/ Amerikanerin (f)*
I don't understand *Ich verstehe Sie nicht*
Where is/are...? *Wo ist/sind...?*
My name is... *Ich heisse...*
At what time? *Wann?*
What time is it? *Wie viel Uhr ist es?*

In the Hotel
Do you have a vacancy? *Haben Sie noch ein Zimmer frei?*
a single room *ein Einzelzimmer*

a double room *ein Doppelzimmer*
with/without bathroom/ shower *mit/ohne Bad/Dusche*

Emergencies
Help *Hilfe*
I need a doctor/dentist *Bitte rufen Sie einen Arzt/Zahnarzt*
Can you help me? *Können Sie mir helfen?*
Where is the hospital?/police station?/telephone? *Wo finde ich das Krankenhaus?/die Polizeiwache?/das Telefon?*

Shopping
Do you have...? *Haben Sie...?*
How much is it? *Wie viel kostet es?*
Do you take credit cards *Akzeptieren Sie Kreditkarten?*
When do you open/close? *Wann machen Sie auf/zu?*
size (clothes) *Kleidergrösse*
size (shoes) *Schuhgrösse*
small change *Kleingeld*
cheap *billig*
expensive *teuer*

Sightseeing
visitor information *Touristen- Information*
exhibition *Ausstellung*
open *geöffnet*
closed *geschlossen*
entry fee *Eintrittspreis*

Menu Reader
I'd like to order *Ich möchte bestellen*
I am a vegetarian *Ich bin Vegetarier (m)/Vegetarierin (f)*
The check, please *Die Rechnung, bitte*
dinner *Abendessen*
menu *Speisekarte*

salt *Salz*
pepper *Pfeffer*
bread *Brot*
cheese *Käse*
wine list *Weinkarte*
water *Wasser*

Drinks *Getränke*
Apfelsaft apple juice
Bier beer
Kaffee coffee
Orangensaft orange juice
Rotwein red wine
Weisswein white wine

Breakfast *Frühstück*
Brötchen bread roll
Eier eggs
Speck bacon

Meat & Fish *Fleisch & Fisch*
Bockwurst large frankfurter
Forelle trout
Krabben shrimp
Lachs salmon
Leberknödel liver dumplings
Rinderbraten roast beef
Sauerbraten marinated beef
Schinken ham

Fruit & Vegetables *Obst & Gemüse*
Apfel apple
Apfelsine/Orange orange
Erdbeeren strawberries
Kartoffeln potatoes
Kohl cabbage
Reis rice
Spargel asparagus
Weintrauben grapes
Zitrone lemon
Zwiebeln onions

Desserts *Nachspeisen*
Apfelkuchen apple cake
Krapfen/Berliner doughnuts
Obstkuchen fruit tart

INDEX

CREDITS

Author

Paul Sullivan

Additional text by: Paul Dowswell, Jan Otakar Fischer, Nicky Gardner, Susanne Kries, and Brendan Nash And with thanks to: David Dörrast, Marc Funde, Dr. Ruth Mandel, Dirk Palme, Mark Ravenhill, and Marie Theurer

Picture Credits

Abbreviations: SS (SuperStock), RH (Robert Harding), DR (Dreamstime.com), SH (Shutterstock)

t = top, b = bottom, l = left, r = right, m = middle

2-3 Luca Da Ros/SIME/4Corners; **4** Malte Jaeger; **5tr** Luca Da Ros/SIME/4Corners; **5bl** AA World Travel Library/Alamy; **5mr** Held Jurgen/age fotostock/RH; **6** Malte Jaeger; **9** Günter Gräfenhain/4Corners; **12-13** Artsy/DR; **14t** fotoVoyager/iStock.com; **15t** Massimo Borchi/SIME/4Corners; **15bm** Günter Gräfenhain/4Corners; **17** Malte Jaeger; **18tl** Maria Heyens/Alamy; **18br** Ben Southgate; **19** Carol_Anne/iStock.com; **20** Lucas Vallecillos/age fotostock/RH; **22bl** Giovanni Simeone/SIME/4Corners; **22t** Malte Jaeger; **23tr** Guido Cozzi/SIME/4Corners; **23br** Marka/SuperStock; **24** Jürgen Henkelmann/imagebrokernet/SuperStock; **26t** RodrigoBianco/iStock.com; **26b** Iain Masterton/age fotostock/RH; **27b** Malte Jaeger; **28** Trabi Safari/East Car Tours GmbH & Co. KG; **30b** Walter G.Allgower/imagebroker/RH; **31tr** Jens Benninghofen/Alamy; **31tl** Christian Reister/imagebroker/RH; **31br** © DDR Museum, Berlin 2014; **33** Konstantinos Papaioannou/DR; **34bl** Miquel Tres Lopez/age fotostock/RH; **34tl** Patrick Poendl/123RF.com; **35bm** National Geographic; **35tr** Ben Southgate; **36** Anna Serrano/SIME/4Corners; **38tm** National Geographic; **38bl** LOXX am ALEX Miniatur Welten Berlin; **39t** LOOK foto/SuperStock; **39b**, 41 RITTER SPORT, Bunte SchokoWelt, Berlin; **42** Adam Eastland/Alamy;

43tl © SDTB/Foto: F. Grosse; **43r** Anticicio/iStock.com; **44** Iain Masterton/Alamy; **46-47** National Geographic; **50** Iain Masterton/age fotostock/RH; **52m** Malte Jaeger; **52bl** Noppasin/SH; **53mr** Walter G.Allgower/imagebroker/RH; **53bm** lexan/SH; **54** Malte Jaeger; **55** National Geographic; **56** marcovarro/SH; **58** © Deutsche Bank KunstHalle; **61** Julie Woodhouse/imagebroker/RH; **62** Zanna Karelina/SH; **64** Gianni Dagli Orti/The Art Archive; 65 John Springer Collection/Corbis; **66** Everett Collection/Rex Features; **67** akg-images; **69** Malte Jaeger; **70** Iain Masterton/Alamy; **72bl** rfarrarons/iStock.com; **72bm** Rainer F.Steussioff/intro/imagebroker/Alamy; **73br** Peter Horree/Alamy; **73tm** John Hicks/Corbis; **74** Jean-Pierre Lescourret/Corbis; **77** Noppasin Wongchum/123RF.com; **79** Uli Deck/epa/Corbis; **81** Iain Masterton/Alamy; **82** National Geographic; **84** (00013020) Margarete Büsing/Ägyptisches Museum und Papyrussammlung, Staatliche Museen zu Berlin/bpk; **85** Ben Southgate; **86** Corbis; **87** imagebroker.net/SS; **89** Günter Gräfenhain/4Corners; **90** Hemis.fr/SuperStock; **91** Travelstock44/LOOK/RH; **92** Malte Jaeger; **94** Manfred Harzl/DR; **95tc** Prisma/Album/akg-images; **95mr** (00022269) Jörg P. Anders/Nationalgalerie, SMB/bpk **96** Karl Johaentges/LOOK/RH; **98** Gary Yim/SH; **100** National Geographic; **102** Svetlana Samarkina/123RF.com; **103** National Geographic; **105** Carsten Koall/Getty Images; **107** Foundation Prussian Palaces and Gardens Berlin-Brandenburg/JTB Photo/SS; **108tr** Stiftung Preußische Schlösser und Gärten Berlin-Brandenburg/photographer: Jörg P. Anders; **108bl** Stefano Amantini/4Corners; **109tl** Emanuele Leoni/DR; **109mr** Hemis.fr/SS; **110** Foto: Monique Wüstenhagen/© The Story of Berlin; **112** Erik De Graaf/DR; **113** Jurgen Henkelmann/imageBROKER/RH; **114** Foundation Prussian Palaces and Gardens Berlin-Brandenburg/Abel Tumik/Dreamstime.com; **116** Foundation Prussian Palaces and Gardens Berlin-Brandenburg/Nomad/

SS; **117** Foundation Prussian Palaces and Gardens Berlin-Brandenburg/Alexandre Fagundes De Fagundes/DR; **118** Frederick II as King (oil on panel), Pesne, Antoine (1683-1757) (attr.to) / Staatliches Schlosser und Garten, Postdam, Germany/The Bridgeman Art Library; **119** akg-images; **121** Sean Gallup/Getty Images; **122** Erich Teister/123RF.com; **124bl** Malte Jaeger; **125tr** Luca Da Ros/SIME/4Corners; **125ml** Massimo Borchi/SIME/4Corners; **125br** Ben Southgate; **126** Hemis.fr/SuperStock; **127** Malte Jaeger; **129** Luca Da Ros/SIME/4Corners; **130** Caro/Alamy; **132** Alvaro Leiva/RH; **133** travelstock44/Alamy; **134** Bread and Butter, Berlin; **135** Schroewig/BP/dpa/Corbis; **137** David Yates/ HYPERLINK "http://andberlin.com" http://andberlin.com; **138** Gianluca Santoni/SIME/4Corners; **140** John Stark/Alamy; **141t** © Jüdisches Museum Berlin, Foto: Jens Ziehe; **141b** Ben Southgate; **142** (10005819) bpk; **143** Juergen Henkelmann Photography/Alamy; **145** © Berlinische Galerie, Photo: Nina Strassguetl; **146** Sammlung Werkbundarchiv – Museum der Dinge, Berlin/Foto: Armin Herrmann; **147** Vin Aqua Vin; **148** Massimo Ripani/SIME/4Corners; **150** Daniela Incoronato; **151** Sean Gallup/Getty Images; **153** Urbanmyth/Alamy; **154** Wolfgang Scholvien; **156l** Agentur Garp Hoppe, Tm/ Deutsche Zentrale für Tourismus e.V.; **156r** I.Haas, Botanischer Garten und Botanisches Museum Berlin-Dahlem; **157** Chodan/AlliiertenMuseum; **158** Bettmann/Corbis; **159** AA World Travel Library/Alamy; **160** Britta Pedersen/dpa picture alliance/Alamy; **162** Paul Sullivan; **164** Colin McPherson/Corbis; **165** Bettmann/Corbis; **166** Zettler/dpa/Corbis; **167** Robert Wallis/SIPA/Corbis; **169** Kuttig – Travel/Alamy; **170** Karl Johaentges/LOOK/RH; **171** Maria Conradi/Caro/Alamy; **172-173** Carlo Moruchio/RH.

Cover: (UP) David Coleman/Alamy; (LO) Shutterstock/Krasowit

Spine: Shutterstock/Artgraphpixel.com

Back cover: Rainer F. Steussioff/intro/imagebroker/Alamy

3/b   6 × 5/18 (1/19)

Walking Berlin

Published by the National Geographic Society
Gary E. Knell, *President and Chief Executive Officer*
John M. Fahey, Jr., *Chairman of the Board*
Declan Moore, *Chief Media Officer*
Chris Johns, *Chief Content Officer*
Keith Bellows, *Senior Vice President and Editor in Chief, National Geographic Travel Media*

Prepared by the Book Division
Hector Sierra, *Senior Vice President and General Manager*
Janet Goldstein, *Senior Vice President and Editorial Director*
Jonathan Halling, *Creative Director*
Marianne R. Koszorus, *Design Director*
Barbara A. Noe, *Senior Editor, National Geographic Travel Books*
Elisa Gibson, *Art Director*
R. Gary Colbert, *Production Director*
Mike Horenstein, *Production Manager*
Jennifer A. Thornton, *Director of Managing Editorial*
Susan S. Blair, *Director of Photography*
Meredith C. Wilcox, *Director, Administration and Rights Clearance*
Marshall Kiker, *Associate Managing Editor*
Judith Klein, *Production Editor*
Marlena Serviss, *Contributor*
Katie Olsen, *Design Production Specialist*
Nicole Miller, *Design Production Assistant*
Bobby Barr, *Manager, Production Services*

Created by Toucan Books Ltd
Ellen Dupont, *Editorial Director*
Anna Southgate, *Editor*
Dave Jones, *Designer*
Palmedia, *Editorial Support*
Merritt Cartographic, *Maps*
Marion Dent, *Proofreader*
Marie Lorimer, *Indexer*

The information in this book has been carefully checked and to the best of our knowledge is accurate. However, details are subject to change, and the National Geographic Society cannot be responsible for such changes, or for errors or omissions. Assessments of sites, hotels, and restaurants are based on the author's subjective opinions, which do not necessarily reflect the publisher's opinion.

The National Geographic Society is one of the world's largest nonprofit scientific and educational organizations. Its mission is to inspire people to care about the planet. Founded in 1888, the Society is member supported and offers a community for members to get closer to explorers, connect with other members, and help make a difference. The Society reaches more than 450 million people worldwide each month through *National Geographic* and other magazines; National Geographic Channel; television documentaries; music; radio; films; books; DVDs; maps; exhibitions; live events; school publishing programs; interactive media; and merchandise. National Geographic reflects the world through its magazines, television programs, films, music and radio, books, DVDs, maps, exhibitions, live events, school publishing programs, interactive media and merchandise. National Geographic has funded more than 10,000 scientific research, conservation, and exploration projects and supports an education program promoting geography literacy. For more information, visit www.nationalgeographic.com.

For more information, please call 1-800-NGS LINE (647-5463) or write to the following address:

National Geographic Society
1145 17th Street N.W.
Washington, D.C. 20036-4688 U.S.A.

For information about special discounts for bulk purchases, please contact National Geographic Books Special Sales: ngspecsales@ngs.org

For rights or permissions inquiries, please contact National Geographic Books Subsidiary Rights: ngbookrights@ngs.org

ISBN: 978-1-4262-1471-4

Printed in Hong Kong
14/THK/1

CREDITS